The Bottom Lines 2019

52 More Important Lessons in Leadership

Tom Zender

Endorsements for Tom Zender's Work

"Tom articulates well the principles necessary to create a business culture and value system that provides the supportive environment for individuals to successfully collaborate, innovate, and deliver great results."
– Fred Anderson, former CFO of Apple Computer

"Tom's understanding of both business success and spiritual values has led him to the knowledge that the two are not separate entities - they are two sides of the same coin, and he deftly shows their integration."
– Deepak Chopra, bestselling author of *The Seven Spiritual Laws of Success*

"Tom Zender is an astute business author and educator. His enlightened work is drawn deeply from his own experiences as a successful business leader. He brings that expertise into the academic world as well. Tom teaches with authenticity and wit."
– Dr. Wendy Campbell, PhD University of Southern California, Professor of Instructional Design for Arizona State University and Capella University

"Tom Zender masterfully raises the consciousness and confidence of people and their organizations."

– Jack Canfield, co-creator of the *Chicken Soup for the Soul* book series; bestselling author of *The Success Principles*

"Zender explains how to leap ahead of the field by taking the most important leap of all: recognizing the power of your inner spirit to create breakthroughs you might not have ever thought possible."
– Marianne Williamson, New York Times bestselling author of *Return to Love*

"You were a distinct asset to General Electric. Your ability to communicate is outstanding."
– Kenneth G. Fisher, former Vice President of General Electric

"You know going in that he's an accomplished business leader and mentor with an impressive record of success and achievements. He's sincere and authentic. He is humble, kind and appreciates being in your company. He's a good listener. If he has an ego, he hides it well. He's a role model leader."
– Don Henninger, former CEO and Publisher, *Phoenix Business Journal*

Dedication

The Bottom Lines 2019: 52 More Important Lessons in Leadership is dedicated to the generous CEO's and business mentors who have enriched my career by sharing their wisdom, providing their unselfish guidance, and by giving their steadfast devotion to my success. I deeply thank you, always.

Also, this book is dedicated to the readers of my weekly column, *Leadership Lessons,* in the digital edition of the *Phoenix Business Journal.* I am indebted to Publisher, Ray Schey; Chief Editor, Gregg Barr; Managing Editor, Patrick O'Grady; and Digital Editor, Tim Gallen. They gave to me the privilege of writing weekly about the key element of all businesses – real leadership.

And, not to forget my cat, Angel, my faithful Muse who inspired me in writing all of my books, including this one.

As always, I am indebted to my wife, Wendy Zender, Ph.D., and so many business friends who have supported me in creating this *The Bottom Lines* series of books.

Table of Contents

Endorsements for Tom Zender's Work

Dedication

Table of Contents

Leadership Lessons 1 - 52

Preface

Acknowledgements

About the Author

Leadership Lessons 1 to 52

 #   Lesson

01 Shut up and listen for solutions in solitude and silence.

02 Seven signs of a toxic workplace and how to clean it up.

03 After a load of losses, how do you bounce back?

04 What sort of leader are you (multiple choice)?

05 No title, no position, yet a leader that others want to follow.

06 The uncomfortable convenience of pretending not to know.

How to Order More Books

Preface

I am a Professional CEO Mentor. I continuously meet great leaders in my work, learning valuable lessons along the way. During my business career, I have collected hundreds of business lessons from my mentors, leaders, clients, and others. These teachings are brief, simple, powerful. And immediately useful.

The Bottom Lines 2019 is devoted to sharing more of the best lessons I have learned from a wide audience of business people: leaders, managers, and you.

Rather than the typical laborious business writings that we encounter, I write in a more conversational way – because I find that business wisdom is easier and more interesting to read and remember. Brevity counts. So does a touch of humor.

My business path began with General Electric and Honeywell, and moved through midsize and startup companies, and a global nonprofit organization. My leadership roles included CEO, senior VP, and board member in Fortune 500, NASDAQ, Toronto Stock Exchange, and other companies.

Today I am a professional CEO Mentor & Business Coach. Additionally, I mentor Arizona State University faculty members and students who have startup businesses, as well as serving the Maricopa County Community College District, the Center for Entrepreneurship and Innovation, the advisory board of Ottawa University's business school. And, I write a weekly column, *Leadership Lessons*, for the Phoenix Business Journal.

I have had a taste of everything on the broad buffet of business. Mostly satisfying. But with some occasional heartburn, too!

The Bottom Lines 2019 includes a wide variety of lessons from different business functions. Above all, they are useful for building better business. Proven stuff.

Each lesson ends with a short summary, *The Bottom Lines.* Here is the one for *Leadership and the five "Laws of Bigness."*

The Bottom Lines

Play big. Follow the Five Laws of Bigness: Vision, Culture, Action, Failure, Results. Your business will be irresistibly attractive, work intensely, build huge momentum, create opportunities from mistakes, and achieve great results. Bigness is better.

Acknowledgements

Thank you, all of my memorable business mentors at General Electric, Honeywell, Ottawa University, and many others.

I am grateful to those mentors who taught me to mentor others as my way of giving away what I learned.

And, yes, I thank my "anti-mentors" who unconsciously convinced me about many attitudes and behaviors that I do not want to emulate. Ever.

I thank hundreds of business writers who have produced the mass of books, articles, columns, and other publications that have so positively influenced me.

Thank you so very much to many business and personal friends for giving me ongoing support to bring *The Bottom Lines Series* of books to business readers who seek new ways to improve their leadership skills.

Thank you to the team at Kindle Direct Publishing and Amazon for their focused and expert assistance to help me to transform this book, and the other books in this series, from a vision into a reality.

Above all, I am forever grateful to my wife, chief supporter, and editor, Dr. Wendy Zender, Ph.D., University of Southern California. Wendy is gifted in helping me transform good ideas into something readable and useful. She should be. She is a graduate university professor who reads a continuous stream of doctoral level theses from her students. I think I am one of them!

About the Author

Tom Zender is a Professional CEO Business Mentor, Coach and Leadership Developer in Phoenix, Arizona.

He held leadership roles at General Electric and Honeywell, and has been a senior vice president in publicly held corporations, New York Stock Exchange and NASDAQ listed. Tom was the CEO of a startup technology company and he was president and CEO of a two million member nonprofit.

His corporate board experience includes NASDAQ, Toronto Stock Exchange, and OTC listed public companies. Tom held nonprofit board positions with Ottawa University and the Forum for Corporate Directors.

In his CEO and senior vice president roles he held profit and loss responsibility for every business function.

Tom mentors faculty and students who have startup businesses at Arizona State University, is an advisor to the business school of Ottawa University and to Paradise Valley Community College. He serves the Maricopa County Community College District's Center for Entrepreneurial Innovation (CEI). Tom is a guest lecturer at Norther Arizona University.

He has spoken to business audiences of over 1,000 people in more than 20 countries.

Tom Zender is a graduate of Ottawa University with a B.A. in Business in focus areas of Leadership, Marketing, and Information Technology.

He writes a weekly column, *Leadership Lessons*, for the Phoenix Business Journal. His first two published books were Amazon bestseller e-books about business ethics:

- *God Goes to Work,* published in 2010 by John Wiley & Sons, was among the top ten e-books in business ethics listed by Amazon.com.

- *One-Minute Meditations at Work*, published in 2011 by Hay House/Balboa Press, was among the top 5% of all e-books sold by Amazon.com.

His next three books, *The Bottom Lines 2016, The Bottom Lines 2017, The Bottom Lines 2018,* are prequels to this book, *The Bottom Lines 2019* – all part of Tom's expanding *The Bottom Lines Series* of books.

Tom's email address is tomzender@me.com and his website is www.tomzender.com.

Leadership Lesson 1

Shut up and listen for solutions in solitude and silence

Quiet! No, not the command of a grade school teacher. But the understanding that great leaders have about the value of solitude. And silence. Our work world is filled with the din of meetings and machinery. The racket of rock and rap, cell phones a-Twitter, and the jackhammer of desperate keyboards. Amplified noise. But leadership effectiveness is muted. Now what?

Hint: Dwight Eisenhower sought solitude with his military generals while gazing at a downpour before going into the successful launch of D-Day - the battle that turned the tide of World War II into an ultimate win for the U.S. and allies. Solitude spelled success.

"The monotony and solitude of a quiet life stimulates the creative mind." – Albert Einstein, German theoretical physicist

What do great leaders do?

A recent Wall Street Journal article notes that solitude gives leaders the chance to "percolate and marinate in their own feelings and to step out of events and locate sacred space where they can reflect upon what's going on inside, thus attaining the moral and emotional conviction necessary to act."

An executive with Charles Schwab & Co. said, "Solitude makes it possible to engage in the mental equivalent of 'stripping away all the cookies' on a computer. Once they're cleared, my mind works better."

Often, the discovery of how to immerse into solitude is synchronous, serendipitous, a moment of grace. A former CEO of Campbell Soup Company stated that working in his garden created a time of beneficial solitude.

Seeking solitude and silence

The purpose of solitude and silence is to give our brain a rest, to allow optimum solutions to emerge within us, and to increase our energy, focus, and creativity. Solitude and silence are practiced by many in a variety of ways. Important: find the way that works best for you and keep using it as a frequent practice. In all cases, be alone:

- Meditation – a universal way to stop our mind-traffic, be alone in silence, relax, more accepting of ourselves and others, and receptive to new ideas.

- Exercise – being so engrossed in workout patterns (especially aerobic) that we have released the distortions of stress and gained more accurate perspectives in our work.

- Prayer – seeking direction from a power greater than ourselves (per Pew Research, 92% believe in God or a universal spirit – and 50% pray at least once a day).

- Contemplation – focusing on something to the point of simply being present in the moment, more self-aware, and allowing serendipitous connections to emerge.

- Walking – getting "lost" in nature, such that we open ourselves up to a relaxing flow of new information that can help strengthen our leadership skills.

- Soft music – listening to meditative sounds is a way that many leaders and others relax, "zone out" (stop thinking), and become more in tune with ourselves.

- Art – painting, drawing, creative writing, sculpting, pottery, weaving, can improve our leadership by giving us more peace, calm, and serenity.

Create your own. If you have a serendipitous revelation of some attractive way to systematically experience the benefits of solitude, do it. Do not wait.

The Bottom Lines

Shhhh. Enjoy the benefits of spending some time alone in quiet. Solitude and silence. Great leaders do it because they know they need it. Meditation, exercise, prayer, contemplation, walking, music, and art are some of the ways to go quiet. Proven.

Leadership Lesson 2

Seven signs of a toxic workplace and how to clean it up

Negative karma. Bad juju. Low mojo. This is the stew of a stagnating organization. Research found that 17% of employees are active trouble makers. Like noxious weeds, they can spoil an otherwise fruitful garden of growth and success – quickly. What do good leaders do?

First, prevent it. Second, remove the weeds before they sprout seeds. Prevention includes an operating culture that promotes satisfied, happy employees. Removing the toxic employees can involve training, coaching, and reassignment – or an exit door when necessary.

"Toxic people defy logic. Some are blissfully unaware of the negative impact that they have on those around them, and others seem to derive satisfaction from creating chaos and pushing other people's buttons." – Travis Bradberry, coauthor of the bestselling book, *Emotional Intelligence 2.0*

Symptoms of the disease

Before trying to squelch poisons in the organization, you must locate the toxic personnel. Here are some conditions to look for:

1. Control issues and power grabs.
2. Constant complaining with no solutions.
3. Drama kings and queens.
4. Those who are more interested in themselves than the team.
5. Spreading rumors, gossiping.
6. Avoiding responsibility and faulting others.
7. Claiming credit for the good work of others.

These are the people who scatter dysfunctional debris into an organization that could otherwise be healthy. These are the carriers of a communicable disease that can kill good teams, organizations, and entire companies. Time to inoculate the environment. But first, one more possible source. Keep reading.

The big apple

Adage: "Don't let one bad apple spoil the rest." Yes, even if it is the boss. Example: high-rider startup, Uber, designed a dream business in the free-lance drivers market. They drove to the #1 market share before competitors could start their engines.

Travis Kalanick, founder and CEO, developed a reputation for uncivilized communications and abrasive behaviors. Degrading and biased. He was terminated by his board when the company bus hit the wall of unacceptability. One of his recorded quotes, "I'm like fire and brimstone sometimes."

Uber damage? Crumpled reputation, board of directors dented, shareholder scrapes. And competitor Lyft has increased their market share from 21.2% to 24.7% in a few months – while Uber's share has braked from 90% to 75% in two years.

Call "Toxin Busters"

No need to terminate people – yet. Here are some proven, practical means to stop the spread of harmful attitudes and behaviors:

- Utilize inside and outside HR expertise to curb unwanted conduct.
- Hold training sessions to reverse negative behaviors.
- Include leaders and managers in the training sessions.
- Avoid publically naming the offenders; do this privately with them.
- Articulate the tangible and intangible costs of toxic behaviors.
- Demonstrate the value of open, interactive conversations and mutual respect.
- Find incentives for employees to be team players that support the organization.
- Provide rewards to the employees who demonstrate exemplary behaviors.

- Offer professional counselors to assist particularly challenging individuals.
- Support the organization with continuous programs for behavioral improvement.

Yes, ultimately terminate employees who cannot or will not change – and create room for promotions and new-hires that will help create a healthy, well-functioning team.

The bottom lines

Beware. Spot toxic behaviors that choke teams, organizations, and companies. A small group of trouble-making employees are likely poisoning others. Build a program to quickly, and then constantly, neutralize damage. Create a culture that engages employees. Watch teams and the business grow. Disease-free.

Leadership Lesson 3

After a load of losses, how do you bounce back?

Loss. One stings a little. Successive losses are depressing. Even strong leaders can be drained of energy and hope. Teams can weaken and competitors can get stronger. It can, and does happen to anyone – even in the best businesses. So how do you recharge your batteries after a sequence of failures?

Hint: don't fake it. You can't hide it from your team – they know. Another hint: don't try to force yourself to recover too quickly – it might make things worse. What to do? Take a little time to process your emotions, and then move ahead as a better leader. Really.

"It's OK if you fall down and lose your spark. Just make sure that when you get back up, you rise as the whole damned fire."
– Colette Werden, branding expert

Recovering from a litany of losses

Acknowledge your feelings – you are human and feel any number of emotions: sad, angry, anxious, depressed, fearful. We are taught by good therapists to simply allow our normal feelings to be present for a little while. Feel them and then watch them evaporate.

<u>Don't beat yourself up</u> – there are many reasons why the losses may not be your fault at all. Conditions, competitors, and karma might be behind it. But if you feel crappy about a cluster of losses, welcome to being a leader.

<u>Admit mistakes</u> – if you made mistakes, what were they? Identify them, understand the reasons for them, and determine ways to avoid them going forward. Sometimes we learn more from our losses than our wins.

<u>Take a break</u> – time off can the emotional trampoline that will bounce you back on track. A short vacation or staycation is a natural resource for a rebound. For many, spending some quiet time can add a better perspective to a situation.

<u>Talk to someone</u> – a significant other can be a good listener. Just don't let them con you out of your honest feelings so that you can allow let them ebb naturally. Talk to another business leader who has experienced many losses. Or use a professional therapist.

<u>Exercise your body</u> – while this might not lessen your honest feelings, it can reduce the stress that you experience from your normal emotions. And eating right, along other healthy habits, will help your challenging (but normal) feelings.

<u>Sleep and rest</u> – ok, so this is harder when we are emotionally charged. Normal. But try for as much as you can get, including cat naps, meditation, and resting in pleasant and quiet places. Eventually you will sleep well again.

Don't do it. Avoid stuffing your feelings with excessive use of mood altering substances, legal or otherwise. Nothing wrong with a glass of wine – something wrong with a bottle of it. Again, these things merely delay normal feelings that need to emerge healthily.

The bouncers

Edison, Disney, Jobs. All fell to multiple defeats before they rebounded into success. Steve Jobs was fired as the leader of Apple, had several failed products, founded another company, Next, rose again a leader of Apple, merged in Next, ran Pixar simultaneously, and created iEverything. Good job, Steve.

The bottom lines

Losses suck. Especially a litany of them. But strong leaders feel the emotions associated with losses. They use appropriate ways to acknowledge and accept normal feelings. Then watch them dissolve. And then bounce back into action as a stronger leader. Naturally.

Leadership Lesson 4

What sort of leader are you (multiple choice)?

No. Not "management style." We are about to describe *Genus Leaderonus* and its chameleon-like adaptation in the evolution of business environments. Oh yes, management styles have been through several shifts over the decades. But leadership has been far less adaptive – or forced to adapt. Why not?

We do not understand the difference between "leadership" and "management." Analogous to the lack of distinction between marketing and sales. Until IBM and others awakened us with their "here we are" marketing sirens of the 1950's and beyond.

Now comes the evolution of leadership.

Leaders and managers uncloaked

The distinctions of leadership and management can be described briefly with ten easy pieces of contrast:

1. Leaders create and communicate the vision; managers follow the vision.
2. Leaders lead people; managers manage processes.

3. Leaders take the first step; managers take the next step.

4. Leaders ask "why" and "what;" managers ask "how" and "when."

5. Leaders align people; managers organize people.

6. Leaders motivate and inspire; managers administrate and control.

7. Leaders mentor, teach, and pull; managers coach, tell, and push.

8. Leaders challenge the status quo; managers work with the status quo.

9. Leaders unleash potential; managers coordinate resources.

10. Leaders build organizations; managers assemble teams.

This does not infer that leaders are better than managers – they are different by design for different purposes. We need them both.

Leadership types and trends

By learning more about several leadership types, we see the predominant themes in leadership today – and their direction:

Dreaming – converting visions into reality by attracting and great people who are drawn by the dream. Clearly a strong trend over several decades. Example: Apple, Inc.

<u>Supporting</u> – putting employees first so that they, in turn, put customers first. Now increasingly taught at the university level. Example: Southwest Airlines.

<u>Processing</u> – keeping things much the same and giving followers rewards for maintaining the business. Less prevalent today. Example: Blockbuster Video.

<u>Magnetic</u> – transforms followers with a kind of revolutionary energy. Engages fast-moving teams to build businesses. Mixed results. Example: Uber.

<u>Democratic</u> – includes the team in making decisions, with strong bi-directional communications. Fairness is key. Still a definite trend. Example: Google.

<u>Enabling</u> – gives power to the team as the team is able to absorb and effectively use it. Strong, two-way trust is a key ingredient. Example: Tesla.

<u>Non-intervening</u> – leaders keep hands off their team after they have granted autonomy to them. Little interaction. Least popular, going away. Example: General Electric.

<u>Mentoring</u> – uses their experience to teach, coach, demonstrate leadership skills to their team. They develop more leaders. This is a clear trend. Example: General Mills.

"Leaders don't create followers; they create more leaders." – Tom Peters, businessman and author.

Mix and match?

Question: can I adopt several of these leadership types to use with my organization? Answer: you not only can, you should!

Then you can apply a given type or types dynamically in any given situation. The rigid *management* styles of the early-mid 1900's (autocratic or egalitarian) gave way to the dynamic ways of the late century (depending on the situation). Now it is time for *leadership* types to evolve dynamically, situationally. New and powerful.

The bottom lines

Leadership. As you increasingly become a leader, learn more about leadership types, their applicability, and their evolution. There has never been a better time to be a better leader. A dynamic leader. In any situation.

Leadership Lesson 5

No title, no position – yet a leader that others want to follow

Supernatural? Maybe. But there are real leaders who have nobody reporting to them. They have no position and no title. Yet people want to follow them, not because they have to, but because they want to. Voluntarily. There is a certain sixth sense about these leaders that others are drawn to, instinctively. Call it an "irresistible attraction."

Good leaders have many positive attributes, skills, and behaviors. We know several: visionary thinker, inspiring speaker, strong listener, positive attitude, team builder, among others. But typically, these leaders have a title and a high-level position.

But what is it that causes people to willingly follow leaders who have no anointed power nor others reporting to them? Keep reading.

Into their persona

Yes, they are honest, have high integrity, are trusting and trustworthy. And they are kind, fair, supportive of others, and interested in people. Too, they lead balanced lives, take care of their families and relationships, and are often involved in their communities.

They are likable, friendly, generous, considerate, respecting and respectable. They are diligent workers and have good records of accomplishments. They care about their employers and the organizations they represent. If not supernatural, they might appear as superhuman.

But all of this is not quite enough to constitute a leader without title or position that others want to follow voluntarily. What is missing?

Into their soul

Authenticity. It is the powerful "magnetic resonance" that attracts and engages other people. It inspires those who are like-minded. We are being authentic when we think, speak, and act from our heart and soul – our true inner self. We are perceived as trusting and trustworthy. This is the real core of the so-called "natural leader."

They may have no title, no position, no staff, no anointed power. Yet, if they take the lead in a business program or project, others will willingly join in. Often, others do not have to be invited. They volunteer.

Authenticity does not answer the question of, "Who am I?" Authenticity affirms, "Who I am."

Softer words, louder actions

Of course, those leaders who do have people reporting to them, titles, positions, and anointed power, can be authentic. They should be. And for long term success, they must be.

Importantly, how do authentic leaders of both kinds behave? They:

- Give others credit, never themselves.
- Treat everyone fairly, consistently.
- Gather input from a wide cross-section of people.
- Admit their faults and failures.
- Build teams that are energized, creative, and durable.
- Serve their employees and bring out the best in them.
- Share rewards with their people.
- Mentor and teach their employees.
- Never criticize; instead they offer professional, constructive input.
- Respect everybody.
- Communicate frequently, and listen carefully.
- Clearly open and honest with great integrity – always.

"Truth is a point of view, but authenticity can't be faked." – Peter Guber, American executive, entrepreneur, educator

Authentic template

Ghandi led the entire country of India in its non-violent separation from British rule. He had no title and no position. Millions of people followed him to freedom. Voluntarily.

The bottom lines

Be a leader. Even if you do not have a title, position, or anointed power. Be authentic and lead from your inner core, consistently. Others will naturally follow you to support your projects because they want to. And, if you do have positional power, all the more reason to be authentic. Always.

Leadership Lesson 6

The uncomfortable convenience of pretending not to know

Later. We'll deal the problem someday. But it is too much to face right now. The unadmitted nagging truth that something is wrong. A product weakness, an encroaching competitor, an employee that isn't performing a critical task. But we'll ignore it and hope that the issue goes away. Pretend that the smoke is not a fire. Why?

Kodak pretended not to know about the relentless encroachment of digital photography. Volkswagen pretended not to know that it had a diesel engine performance deficiency. NASA pretended not to know about the flawed O-rings that downed the Challenger space flight. All brutally costly. Lives, money, reputations.

"The facts remain long after they have been ignored." – Anonymous

What's the motive, anyway?

Why would a leader (or anyone else) ignore warning signs of an existing or pending serious problem? Here is a short list of reasons:

Distancing – not wanting to be identified with the problem; or worse, be seen as the cause of it. Keeping "one's skirt clean."

Laziness – believing that it is not worth the effort to deal with the issue; it is better to use resources on non-problems.

Pollyannaism – "everything is fine, nothing is wrong;" turn our heads the other way and pretend the problem does not exist.

Wishful thinking – the concern will resolve itself and go away; someone else will see the issue and take care of it.

Minimization – this concern is really small and not worth worrying about; it cannot do much damage and we have more important things to do.

Cost – we have limited financial resources and should not waste them on fixing a problem instead of spending on more important tasks.

Time – it will take too long to fix the issue and that will delay the entire project too much. Management will reward us for staying on track.

The above reasons, and many more, are meant to justify our "pretending not to know" – but in our intuitive hearts and souls we know that something is very wrong and should be corrected. Fast.

And what do real leaders do?

Facts. Get facts, face facts, deal with facts, take action. This is a time to take time for some risk analysis to determine the worst that could happen, and the likelihood of it happening. Determine all costs, such as money, time, reputations, and lost business.

The brave hide nothing, get everything out in the open, energize teams, ask for help, and lay out plans to resolve the challenge. And then implement the plan. Forcefully.

Communicate problems and progress to eliminate surprises for everyone concerned. Admit the problem at the beginning – and announce the solution at the end.

Will the real costs please stand up?

At the beginning of this writing, three examples were given of problems that were effectively "swept under the rug." Here are the known costs:

Kodak – bankruptcy, broken up, assets and patents sold off.

Volkswagen – $20B in fines and fees, stock price down 20%, reputation mangled.

NASA – seven astronauts lost, billions of dollars wasted, program delayed three years.

"Pretending Not to Know" is a deadly game that only the foolish play.

The bottom lines

Convenient, maybe – uncomfortable, always. Failing to address problems can be brutally costly. As true leaders, take the high watch and address real and potential problems face-on. Fast. In the long run, save time, costs, reputations, businesses. And sometimes lives.

Leadership Lesson 7

The ten deadly diseases of a business and how to heal them

Illness. A corporate body can be sick. Just like a human body. And so can small-medium business and nonprofit bodies. The symptoms of an ailing business must be diagnosed. People can die of illness. Likewise businesses. Sometimes quickly.

A good business might have grown strongly with leadership and staffing, innovative products and services, and profitable growth. Everything may look healthy, but there could be subtle, increasing internal discomforts.

Good news: there can be financial indicators of a sick business. Bad news: often the financial results are lagging indicators. What are the leading indicators?

Open wide and say "ah"

Here are the critical symptoms of an ailing business:

<u>Leaderitis</u>
The leader of a business has stopped leading. There is a weakening of vital functions that create a good business: vision,

mission, values, strategy and execution. It is time to resuscitate the business and return it to good health.

Depression

Apathy, loss of energy, and its companion "we do not have any competitors" are deadly. Leaders must re-awaken themselves and the organization with an injection of newness, excitement, and passion.

Weak extremities

A once-vibrant organization can suffer from poor hiring practices and retaining non-performing employees. It is time to reevaluate the team and transplant weak players with outstanding new people. Upgrade and good employees and reward them.

Geriatric issues

Products and services are no longer viable in the market. Product engineering and production planning are not in rhythm and move too slowly. Do reinforce good teamwork in marketing, development, and production. Bring new products to market, fast.

Poor eyesight

Standards and controls are not defined nor practiced. Important information is too slow. Do articulate expectations and compare actual performance against established standards.

Communicate results and celebrate a return to good business health.

Recurring dizziness

Markets are changing quickly and customer bases are muddled. The marketing organization is out of touch. Products are out of date. Stop the spinning chaos by getting good market data and building strong marketing and sales programs.

Clogged arteries

Customers are not respected and receive bad service. There is little effort to understand their true needs. Insist that the sales and service organizations are trained to care for customers above all. It costs more to get a new customer than to keep an existing one.

Malnutrition

There is insufficient cash from loans, investors, sales, and other means to support growth. Develop a plan and to generate cash and attract investments. It is easier to get capital before you need it. Always hoard cash and have it available for opportunities.

Irregular heartbeat

Information technology is old, complicated, and fails to support the business. Training and procedures are not aligned with IT. Upgrade IT so that it best fulfills its essential role in supporting the business. Constantly upgrade IT.

<u>Undetected tumor</u>

There is a false belief that whatever has worked in the past will continue to do so. Failure to change is a top reason that businesses shrink and go under. Prepare to constantly diagnose the business for weak spots and fix them.

Don't ignore any of these symptoms at the risk of losing revenues. Or the business.

The bottom lines

Not feeling well? Before calling an ambulance, start doing frequent checkups on the health of the business. Spot early symptoms of failure before financial reports state that it is too late. Be well.

Leadership Lesson 8

The new think, talk, listen, act ratios

Not financial ratios. We are looking at behavioral ratios that feed financial ratios. Financial ratios include gross margin, return on equity, current ratio, and more. Communications ratios include think/talk ratio, talk/listen ratio, talk/act ratio, and more. Why is this important?

Understanding the dynamics of our communications is key to improved performance and productivity. If we do not think before we talk, or listen as much as we talk, or act more than we talk, we are feeding weak financial performance.

Keep reading.

What are you thinking?

Business performance weakening. Management and employees are thinking about it. But not much else. Here is what they should be thinking about. What is important now?

1. Review the entire business: vision, mission, values, goals, strategy, actions, results.

2. Isolate all the weak spots via conversations, questions, and listening.

3. Carefully think through the priorities of what needs to be done.

"You must do the things you think you cannot do." – Eleanor Roosevelt, First Lady of the United States, 1933-1945

Engage brain before releasing tongue

From thought to tongue is a split-second. So fast that we too often say things that we do not mean. Or in a manner that we would like to retract. Add the fact that we like to talk more than listen – and speak more than taking action – and our vocal chords become more of a liability than an asset. What to do?

1. Make a mental list of some things you want to talk about.
2. Take a breath or two before starting to speak to consciously form your first sentence.
3. Talk slowly so that you can continue to manage your feelings and words.

"Wise people speak because they have something to say; fools because they have to say something." – Plato, Greek philosopher

Shut up and listen

We are a nation of talkers. But recent *Harvard University* research notes that we should listen two or more times than we talk. Why? Simple. We listen much speedier than we talk. We typically listen and comprehend at 300 WPM (words per minute) while a typical speaker talks at 100 WPM. Easy listening. How?

1. Make eye contact with whoever is talking.
2. Indicate that you are listening by periodically nodding your head.
3. Allow speakers to finish completely prior to you saying anything.

"If we were supposed to talk more than we listen, we would have two tongues and one ear." – Mark Twain, author and humorist

Blah, blah, blah

Are we collectively admiring our problems? By just talking about them? We agree repeatedly that our challenges require action. Yet, we sit in endless meetings with no actions, no assignments, no responsibilities, and no due dates. Now what?

1. Find experienced leaders who will form highly motivated and rewarded teams.
2. Establish meaningful meetings that efficiently drive actions to completion.

3. Stop meetings without a leader, agenda, action lists, or that last more than one hour.

"Leadership is practiced not so much in words as in attitude and in actions." - Harold S. Geneen, American businessman, president and CEO of ITT.

The bottom lines

Communications ratios. What are yours? Are you thinking, listening, talking, and acting in the right proportions. This is critical to building strong financial ratios. Make certain that talking is not your primary company asset. Or it will become your only asset. Soon.

Leadership Lesson 9

Upon reading (and hearing) the fine print

Four-point font. High-speed, low-volume words. Leaders might have a feeling that someone is trying to cover over important information. Leaders might be right. Notice barely legible fine print at the bottom of advertising in print and pixels. Hear announcers read the fine print at unintelligible speeds and unrecognizable volumes. Why?

In legal documents, the writer might prefer that you ignore certain information that could block the signing of a contract. Obscurity is their friend.

Leaders and others are high-speed people in a high-speed world. Who has time to deal with a mass of fine print – written or spoken?

Step up to the bar

The legal profession plays a key role in fine print. Creating it and interpreting it. If you need help understanding the fine print, including what you are hearing, ask for legal help.

There is a legal technicality that demands full disclosure – the good, the bad, and the ugly – of the terms and conditions associated with the advertised product. However, that legal requirement does not require any particular font size.

The mere presence of fine print can psychologically fool the reader of the larger print into the belief that the product offer is more favorable than it truly is – even though significant evidence suggests that most readers do not read the fine print.

Sleight of hand and mouth

Get this: fine print can actually state the opposite of the large print. E.g., the large print might say, "pre-approved," but the fine print could state, "subject to approval." Big difference.

Drug company fine print (written and spoken) often contain warnings. But the colorful artwork, videos, and spoken messages in the advertising deflects readers, viewers, and listeners from paying attention to the fine print.

The Federal Trade Commission requires that the terms of advertised offers must be legally stated conspicuously and clearly. Yet, advertisers put fine print in camouflaged colors or verbally spoken quickly and softly. A challenge for readers and listeners to understand.

Caveat emptor (buyer beware)

Oh yes – sellers and buyers need to be aware of fine print, too. Doing a huge business deal. Buying or selling a house. Same issues. How is the deal affected by the fine print? Hug a lawyer.

Consumers are particularly vulnerable. Be aware and beware of these kinds of phrases in fine print:

<u>Exclusions apply.</u> This detail may appear with an itemized list of products that are excluded from the advertised deal. Note carefully.

<u>Not valid in conjunction with…</u> Retailers will be restrictive about what coupons can be combined with which promotions. In other words, read and understand the fine print.

<u>Minimum purchase of…</u> Gift certificates often require the holder to purchase at least a given amount. Or to consume restaurant food by dining in, not take-out. Read twice.

<u>Not Valid on…</u> Found a great deal on airline tickets? Before you purchase, look deeply for all restrictions. Certain days and time, certain classes of travel. Caution.

"Education is when you read the fine print; experience is what you get when you don't." – Pete Seeger, American musician.

The bottom lines

Read. See. Hear. Good leaders (and others) do not ignore the fine print. On a printed page, in a video, or audio from radio or TV ads. From corporate contracts to consumer information. Love a lawyer or understand it yourself. Avoid legal and financial disappointments. And disasters.

Leadership Lesson 10

Interpersonal relationships and the leadership of everything

Why bother? Look at the cost of employees bonding in their workplace. Worse than that, look at the higher cost of not having employees who value interpersonal relationships. Oh, and not all managers have good interpersonal skills. Hmmmmm.

"Leaders" without interpersonal relationship skills are not really leaders. In recent Harvard University research, the top seven skills of strong leaders are based upon their ability to foster good interpersonal relationships with and among their people.

The old authoritarian, dictatorial, hierarchical, tell-do model of management is gone. After ruining a number of corporations. Try "Chainsaw" Al Dunlap and the near murder of the Sunbeam Corporation. He was sued by the SEC and barred from ever again serving as an officer or director of a public company.

And what is it?

Interpersonal relationships are defined as the strong association between employees working together in the same organization – creating a positive, productive work environment.

What are the top seven skills of the best business leaders?

1.   Inspiring and motivating others.
2.   Displaying high integrity.
3.   Solving problems.
4.   Driving for results.
5.   Communicating powerfully and prolifically.
6.   Promoting and celebrating teamwork.
7.   Builds relationships.

The point is that it is beyond difficult to achieve these skills without a durable foundation of first building great interpersonal relationships.

Everybody stand up

Here are people from the office, production, and other parts of your work environment to include in building powerful interpersonal connections and bonding:

Peers, employees, customers and prospects, members of the surrounding community, vendors, media, managers, supervisors, leaders, teammates, visitors, collaborators, board members, directors, investors. In other words, everybody.

In his classic book, "How to Win Friends and Influence People," American motivational writer and speaker Dale Carnegie noted, "You can make more friends in two months by becoming interested in other people than you can in two years by trying to get other people interested in you."

How is it done?

Employees must communicate with each other effectively for a healthy relationship. Remember that a problem shared is a problem halved. Take the time to interact with your co-workers more often. Face-to-face meetings create deeper personal bonding, but phone calls, and well-written emails can work. Texts, too.

Even employees from a different team can be your friends. Informal meetings can lower barriers and open up pathways to deeper interpersonal relationships. Bring coffee, allow informal conversation. Remember to listen a lot. Others like to be heard and it builds mutual trust and caring. FYI, we learn more when we listen than when we talk.

Have some food together. Celebrate wins together. Appreciate someone who has performed exceptionally well. Stand by your colleagues when needed – help someone. Especially through a challenge.

It's all about relationships

Yes, there are immense benefits to building great interpersonal relationships:

- Interactions are improved in our workplaces.
- We make better decisions.
- The culture is improved.
- We gain support from others.
- Teams are strengthened.
- The power of friendship is unlocked.

And our work is easier and more productive in a culture of genuine friendships. Smile.

The bottom lines

Relationships. Every good leader knows the power of strong working relationships. And these leaders help their organizations do the same. Build durable friendships throughout the company. And beyond. Enjoy a culture of working relationships. See the organization glow. And the business grow.

Leadership Lesson 11

The (not so) invisible entrepreneurs

Where are they? The creative leaders and entrepreneurs that risk big to start new businesses? Universities, tech incubators, geographic startup hotspots, corporate labs, startup accelerators, and others. Who else?

Community colleges. They are emerging contributors to new ventures. One million associate degrees are granted yearly in the United States, mostly by community colleges. University-granted bachelor degrees number two million annually. So, community colleges are contributing about one-third of these foundational degrees.

And, community colleges are helping with the creation of some 500,000 new U.S. businesses each month. Amazing.

Out of the desert

Paradise Valley Community College (PVCC) in Phoenix is part of the largest community college system in the United States. The Maricopa County Community College District serves some

200,000 students with ten colleges and a new venture accelerator.

PVCC President, Dr. Paul Dale, is excited to share two exciting programs currently available at PVCC:

1. The Emerging Leadership Program, a nationally recognized leadership program on campus, is designed to teach students to develop a greater understanding of leadership skills, ultimately empowering students to lead and believe in their ability to make a difference.

2. The Entrepreneurial Program is a new certificate program that serves to educate students to acquire the skills to start their own venture. President Dale and his team realize that successful businesses (including startups) require strong leadership abilities.

The two programs have been growing and provide the catalyst for the infusion of creativity in the northeast area of Phoenix. The Emerging Leaders Program has positively influenced local community leaders and nonprofit boards. The Entrepreneurial Certificate has provided many students with the ability to evaluate business startup opportunities, create business plans, and secure a healthy financial future.

Personal proof

In 20 years, over 1,500 students have graduated from Paradise Valley Community College's Emerging Leadership Program.

Here is the story of one graduate, Wendy Shepherd, President and owner of Voices Empowered: Child & Family Advocacy, Investigation and Violence Prevention.

"I was in my late 30's and no further education since high school. I was married at age 18 and spent my early adult life at home raising children. My husband was abusive and we divorced, I was pregnant and wound up with three little kids plus a newborn. I was working 60 hours a week for $6 an hour, receiving no child support, and was not able to pay my bills. My life was difficult. Someone suggested that I go to college and get a grant for support. I learned about PVCC's Emerging Leadership Program, enrolled in it, and I felt loved and supported. What I learned at PVCC was invaluable – that I could be a leader no matter what my circumstances were. I learned that with the right help and support I could make a life for myself and my children. I also have a business where I run a safe house for women. So, my life has come full circle!"

The Paradise Valley Community College Emerging Leadership Program as well as the Entrepreneurial Certificate Program continue to expand the lives of its graduates and those they serve. Entrepreneurship with a heart.

The bottom lines

Aware. Be aware that the U.S. community colleges are an important part of our entrepreneurial and innovation ecosystem. If business leaders want to be involved in
startups at a local level, community colleges are a good place to start. Smart.

Leadership Lesson 12

The "Daily Drowning" and how to resuscitate the victim

Help! I am drowning in too much to do today – and every day. My to-do list is long, I have too much on my plate. Stressed out, bummed out, worn out.

This too much activity every day is contributing to excessive worry and stress and (paradoxically) lowering productivity – the productivity of yourself and the organization.

Who created your to-do list? "They did." Sorry, but you did. Every time. Self-imposed burnout.

Super Woman and Bat Man

If you can accept that you are not a super-hero and are willing to make some simple changes in your workday, there is hope for you and your team.

The key reason you are drowning in the Pool of Too Much is right in front of you: can't say "no," cannot prioritize, do not delegate effectively, and you equate busyness to effectiveness.

There is hope. Read on.

4-S organization

"Stop, Shelve, Send, Start" is your new management mantra. A solution to cut the length of your to-do list and stop your "daily drowning." Every morning, do the following

- Stop as many things in your list as possible. Keep what is really important. Eliminate everything else for your own good and the good of your team.
- Shelve ideas that are good, but there are no resources to work on them. You cannot, and others should not. Review them again later.
- Send the parts of your list that someone else can do to those who can take care of them for you – delegation. Follow up to ensure that these items are being done.
- Start are the remaining things in your (now much shorter) list that you can start doing. Do these things and you will be a better leader.

You are on your way to end your daily drowning. You are resusitated. Breathe.

Important, urgent, and neither

"We are so busy doing the urgent that we do not have time to do the important." – Confucious, Chinese leader, c. 500 BCE.

Ergo, checking email overrides getting high-priority actions done.

Steven Covey wrote it in his classic book, "The Seven Habits of Highly Effective People. General Dwight Eisenhower modeled it in WWII with his four-quadrant "Eisenhower Box."

Good leaders can adopt the "Important/Urgent" quadrant and mentor it into the organization as a effective means of determining what to do. Google "Eisenhower Box" or "Eisenhower Matrix" to learn more. Productive stuff.

Ruthless elimination

Another leader, investor guru Warren Buffet, has an easy method of prioritizing our "Daily Drowning List:"

1. Make a list of the top 15 to 25 things to do.
2. Circle the Top 5 and rank them.
3. Hide all the other items and do not think about them – ruthlessly.
4. Start with the first of the Top 5 and complete it.
5. Then do numbers 2, 3, 4, 5 in order until each one is finished.
6. Now look at the list you hid and choose the next Top 5 (and hide the list again).
7. Repeat as necessary (it is always necessary).

Warren Buffet is worth $50 billion and one of the worlds wealthiest and most respected business people. Simple.

The bottom lines

Don't drown. In your over-filled daily plate of things to do. Use the Stop, Shelve, Send, Start method of shortening your list. Or the "Eisenhower Matrix." Or the Buffett Ruthless Elimination process. Take charge of your leadership time. And effectiveness. Simplify.

Leadership Lesson 13

Scatter-Gather planning for business

Options. We want strategic and actionable options in our planning. Developing those options has been left largely to the Ancient Gods of Brainstorming. There is another more contemporary way to build business planning options. It is your brain trust and 3M Post-it sticky notes. Huh?

Who is your brain trust? Your trusted team, direct and indirect reports, groups of experts in given areas internal people, external people, vendors, boards, and others. And some 3M Post-It "Sticky Notes." Add a meeting room with a big whiteboard, and a neutral facilitator. And someone to build a summary spreadsheet of the meeting.

Like farming, we are about to scatter seeds of business creativity, and then gather up the harvest. Are you kidding? No.

Scatter

Have a half-day meeting. Invite no more than 10 key people with functional strengths from the organization. E.g., engineering, marketing, finance, others. Shut off all cell phones and allow one computer for the note-keeper. Choose a good meeting facilitator. Follow these steps to scatter the emerging ideas onto the whiteboard:

1. Someone outlines a single strategic or actionable issue. Remember that strategy is about "what to do" to do and actions (tactics) are about "how to do it." Example: should we launch this proposed new product and, if so, how best to do it?

2. One or more people familiar with the issue provide a set of facts about the strategic issue – not guesses, innuendo, nor biased opinions. But allow the audience to ask clarifying questions about the issue. No rendering of opinions. Yet.

3. Give everyone a different colored pad of "Sticky Notes." Now, call for 30-minutes of silence while everyone writes out their ideas, one idea per sticky paper. Keep writing – ideas, not opinions.

4. To scatter, the facilitator asks each attendee to go to the whiteboard and paste their sticky notes on it. And, to briefly explain their thinking behind each of their notes. Again, no opinions from either the presenter or the audience.

5. When everyone is finished pasting their notes on the whiteboard and explaining them (briefly), give each member

of the audience a few moments to ask the others for any necessary clarifications.

Now, all the many ideas are scattered on the whiteboard, explained and clarified. The attendees are itching to offer their opinions? Get ready.

Gather

Here are the steps to Gather, organize, and prioritize strategic and actionable ideas:

6. The facilitator begins to rearrange the sticky notes on the board by various categories, inviting the audience to participate in the process. Oh, yes, and now they can make comment, offer opinions, and help the process.

7. Categories can be in a number of ways: by functions, such as marketing, engineering, finance, production, other; by future dates; by available resources.

8. When the facilitator (with help from the audience) clusters the notes by categories, it is critical to establish priorities.

When the process is completed, the result is sent to everyone present and appropriate others in a spreadsheet. Next step – implementation! Otherwise, why bother!

The bottom lines

Scatter ideas. Gather direction. For both strategies and actions. Conduct productive meetings by scattering attendees' ideas onto a whiteboard via "sticky notes." Have attendees discuss, gather related stickies into groups, and prioritize them. Record the results and share them. Don't forget to act on the best ideas. It matters.

Leadership Lesson 14

Constriction, delegation, and the road to empowerment

Stuck. Too slow. Things are not getting done quickly enough. Truth is that things are not getting started soon enough. Staffing is strong, productivity is low. What is wrong? You are not utilizing that strong staff. Why not?

You don't trust others, you think you are the only one that can do it right, everyone else is too slow. Yet you have a killer workload yourself. Take a relaxative. You need to delegate work to others.

Hint: delegation is only a subset of another leadership tool – e.m.p.o.w.e.r.m.e.n.t.

What's that?

Empowerment gifts employees and others the right to take charge of their roles and responsibilities so that they can manage their resources efficiently and effectively, help themselves and others to meet their objectives and attain their goals.

Trust, honesty, and understanding are key behaviors that support the skill of empowering others – including delegating effectively. It is a two-way street for both those doing the delegating, and for those accepting the delegation.

Trust to believe in each other, honesty about what is to be done and the ability to do it, and understanding of the tasks, timeframes, resources involved.

Empowerment is not …

Micromanaging, which is the dead opposite of empowerment, and a killer of effective delegation. Not giving people the leeway to accomplish the work in ways that work for them to achieve the right results.

Intimidating employees to the point of them resisting taking on work for you. Or causing them to hurry and perform sloppily, badmouthing you to others and damaging team morale.

Viewing employees only as robotic tools to generate cash, rather than valuable humans who are equal members of a winning team. They are the ones who can overcome significant challenges and solve problems without you. Surprise!

The empowering leader

Good leaders foster powerful empowerment with these kinds of behaviors:

1. Do not be a babysitter: give employees reasons and opportunity to stretch out on their own and even lead others. They become stronger.

2. Applaud effort: empowered people want greater satisfaction than just money. They want leaders to appreciate their good work. Just say, "Thank you."

3. Ask questions: "How can we add to production?" "How can we improve quality?" "What do you think we should do about this?" Don't debate; decide later.

4. Seek end results: urge empowered employees solve the problem. Specify the end goal so that the team does not solve a different problem. Clarity counts.

5. Set constraints: set limits of time, money and other resources. Ask for reasonable milestones, and review them periodically. This encourages team creativity.

Be positive. Focus on finding and emphasizing what is right, not what's wrong. Be supportive. Don't grab control. And some humor oils the process. Smile.

Read this

Gallup's 2013 Employee Engagement Survey reviewed 1.4 million employees in 50,000 work units. Those companies that empower their employees within good employee engagement practices experience:

- 22% better profitability
- 21% more productivity
- 37% less absenteeism
- 41% fewer quality defects

Plus, improved customer ratings and significantly lower staff turnover. Remarkable.

The bottom lines

Let go, let them. Empower your able staff. Begin by delegating effectively, then expand into broader empowerment. Benefit from more employee and customer satisfaction, stronger teamwork, improved productivity. And lighten your own workload. Smart.

Leadership Lesson 15

Micromanager, empowerer, not sure?

Who me? A micromanager? Never; I empower my people. The micromanager has been long cast as the villain, so no one wants to be labeled as one. The business heroes are the empowerers, and so everyone is a self-acclaimed one. So you think.

Problem. As measured by annual Gallup surveys, over 50% of the U.S. workforce is dissatisfied with their job situation; they are actively disengaged. It is less about pay, the nature of the work, and other employees. It is more about a negative culture. Why?

"People leave managers, not companies." – Anonymous

Meet the Micromanager

Here is the one of the greatest causes of employee dissatisfaction. The micromanager. After reading the following, do you want to be one? Worse, do you want to work for one?

- Micromanagers must know where employees are and what they are doing, always.
- Micromanagers believe that they can do every job better than their employees.
- Micromanagers push all blame for everything to the employees.
- Micromanagers are feared by their employees.
- Micromanagers cause their employees to feel depressed.
- Micromanagers over-assert their authority.
- Micromanagers are controlled by their stress.
- Micromanagers don't know their numbers or value what their employees are creating.
- Micromanagers do not complete regular performance reviews with their employees.
- Micromanagers impose very task-oriented roles for employees.
- Micromanagers provide training that is rigid about how things must be done.
- Micromanagers are reluctant about delegating tasks to employees.
- Micromanagers see vulnerability as a weakness.
- Micromanagers, when they do delegate, dictate how a task is to be done.
- Micromanagers view their employees as robots to make money.
- Micromanagers are not leaders – they are poor managers at best.

This is why productivity is low, turnover is high, and employees are disengaged. What to do?

Enter the Empowerer

Empowering employees builds great teams that enjoy their leaders, the work environment, and being part of something good.

- Empowerers lift and excite their employees.
- Empowerers celebrate wins by acknowledging individuals and teams, regularly.
- Empowerers encourage their employees to identify problems and help solve them.
- Empowerers accept accountability for their own failures and don't blame employees.
- Empowerers describe clearly what they want their people to produce.
- Empowerers will negotiate milestone dates with what is to be delivered and when.
- Empowerers will see vulnerability as a real strength for themselves and employees.
- Empowerers manage stress well for themselves and their teams.
- Empowerers delegate effectively with clarity and mutual commitment.
- Empowerers provide regular performance reviews with their employees.

- Empowerers review programs and projects for progress, helping the teams improve.
- Empowerers are approachable by their people.
- Empowerers do not play favorites.
- Empowerers mentor, coach, teach and promote their people.
- Empowerers value employees for their creativity and problem-solving skills.
- Empowerers are true leaders and highly respected.

Empowerment has proven to be the standard for great leadership. And success.

Say more about the benefits

1.4 million employees in 50,000 locations were surveyed by Gallup in 2013. The organizations that empower their employees benefit from:

- 22% better profitability.
- 21% more productivity.
- 37% less absenteeism.
- 41% fewer quality defects.
- Greater employee engagement.

"Micromanage processes, not people." – Anonymous

The bottom lines

Stop micromanaging. Start empowering. Don't treat employees as robots to make money. Value them for their creativity, and for their ability to prevent problems and to solve issues. Be an empowering leader and enjoy the results. Proven.

Leadership Lesson 16

If you are not giving back, mentor someone

If you are not giving back, mentor someone

Gifts? What did your best mentors give to you? Hands on advice, expert teacher, trusted guidance, a sounding board, devoted support for your career? They were always available, authentic, and open. Thank them. Give back what you received. Mentor someone.

What your good mentors did not do: force their ideas on you, demand that you follow their inputs, fail to listen to you, scold you, ask you to do anything contrary to your values, or do favors for them. If they did, they were not a true mentor.

"The delicate balance of mentoring someone is not creating them in your own image, but giving them the opportunity to create themselves." – Steven Spielberg, American film director, producer, screenwriter

Who might you mentor?

Frequently, we can mentor someone in our workplace. Even a person who reports to us. Others may be in different parts of the organization. Perhaps someone will ask you. Don't announce it, but without forcing yourself just start acting like a mentor to someone who seems interested.

Another opportunity includes your peers. Others in the organization who do not have your experience or abilities. They may need more job instruction, moral support, direction, and other success factors that you can provide.

Consider mentoring those who are facing career challenges or considering a change of jobs. Your guidance could help them avoid unnecessary risks. Or maximize an opportunity. You will feel fulfilled.

5 tips for effective mentoring

Approach each of your mentees differently – none of them are the same. Some important things to remember:

1. Create a mentoring relationship – understand your own readiness and interest. Choose someone to mentor and get to know each other. Build trust, set some goals, and keep the interaction moving forward.

2. Ask more than you answer – don't dive in and spit out all the answers to their questions. Do probe and push, don't

pontificate. Mentees learn more when they create ideas themselves. And model the answers.

3. Be an active listener – engaged listeners are attentive, take notes, ask questions, and repeat back to made certain they have heard properly. Because mentors and mentees spend time listening to each other.

4. Take a personal interest – responsible mentors are invested in the success of their mentees. These mentors are compassionate, knowledgeable, and are good teachers. Good mentors empower their mentees to develop their own strengths.

5. Be positive - shout strongly with optimism and stay silent with criticism. If a mentee has an unrealistic idea, first consider why the idea might work, before you consider why it might not.

A good example

Intel operates a program to match employees with mentors based on the mentees' interest and skills. 25 years ago, Intel became the largest chip maker by revenues and has held that position continuously.

Benefits

There are numerous benefits to being a good mentor (and leader):

- Retain great talent in the organization.
- Get younger talent up to speed faster.
- Expand your own network.
- Learn from your mentees (even the younger ones).
- Increase your sense of purpose.

Mentors feel energized by interacting with their younger and newer associates.

The bottom lines

Give back. Be a better leader by being a good mentor. Offer yourself to a willing candidate in your organization. Help them with their career and enjoy the many benefits. Remember your great mentors and what they did for you. Return the favor. Soon.

Leadership Lesson 17

Scrambled? Seeing details, prioritizing everything, organizing work

Disorganized? Blame the Internet, blame accelerating competitors, blame high-speed buyers, blame complexity. Oooops – blame yourself. Odds are that you and your team are not well organized. Why not?

Not knowing how to organize well. Not seeing the depth of everything that needs to be done, having little sense of effective prioritization, and the self-deception that everything will work itself out.

"Organizing is what you do before you do something, so that when you do it, it is not all mixed up." – A. A. Milne, English author of "Winnie-the-Pooh"

Organizing is …

Skill. Good organizing must be learned and practiced. It is supported by some important behaviors; looking at fine details and prioritizing e-v-e-r-y-t-h-i-n-g.

Organizing pays attention to the purpose, vision, mission, values, and goals of the enterprise. And, especially strategy. Because strategy is the optimum use of limited resources in a competitive setting. Hello business.

What to organize? Not just people in the too-often rigid "Org Chart." Increasingly, human beings in flexible teams. Organize materials, and processes. Oh, and why not first organize your thoughts?

People, materials, processes, info

Here are proven keys to good organization:

<u>People</u>
1. Organizing people is the most important – all else depends upon it.
2. Organizational structures can be vertical (traditional), e.g., production.
3. Other structures can be flatter, e.g., marketing.
4. Flexible organizations adapt dynamically – including self-organizing teams.
5. Teams can be created around a specific task (such as a new product testing).

<u>Materials</u>
1. Build and maintain a list of all materials you think you will need and prioritize it.

2. Include non-production items.

3. Understand deeply why you need the material and when.

4. Costs are a factor, but quality, delivery, terms, conditions, the vendor, matter.

5. Use IT tools to help manage materials.

<u>Processes</u>

1. Utilize cross-functional teams to define processes, including interrelationships.

2. Startups will be more informal.

3. Do it ahead of fast growth when formalization must take place.

4. Not just production – can be any function (sales, customer service).

5. Document for training, organizational changes, business changes.

And, remember that good organization is not micromanagement; it is a continuous process and requires both seeing the details and focusing on priorities.

Details, focus, benefits

Dig into the details deeply with everything. Product designs, testing, production, support. Bookkeeping, accounting, finance – bad data equals bad decisions. Marketing and sales strategies. Everywhere. Adage: God lives in the details. So does the devil.

Prioritize everything. Yup, people, materials, processes, information. Never stop. Use teams to help prioritization. Don't use "High, Medium, Low" priorities – force rank from top to bottom, else everything winds up a "High" priority.

Benefits: delegation becomes more effective, operations are clarified, productivity is increased, costs are lowered, quality is increased, teamwork is improved, less stress resources are optimized, less stress, and leadership is improved. Is that enough?

Amazing example

A former employee describes it as a "well-organized" company. It has always been that way. Their stunning success has dramatically changed our world. Amazon is *Forbes 2017 #2* most admired company in the U.S. A well-organized Apple is #1.

The bottom lines

Get organized. People, materials, processes. Get your team involved. Dig into all the details. Prioritize everything always. Enjoy all the benefits by starting now. Do more with less. Guaranteed.

Uncertainty and navigating the unknown regions of business

Certainty. We want it, but too often cannot have it. Fast breaking changes, external forces, and unpredictable results foil our expectations. And our careful planning. What goes wrong?

When we leave little room for errors in our planning, we are striving for certainty. Better that we consider an improved method of planning – and managing our expectations about outcomes.

"If there's one thing that's certain in business, it's uncertainty." – Stephen Covey, author of the bestseller, *The Seven Habits of Highly Effective People*.

What if?

Launching a strategic business plan with no leeway for unexpected changes is like a running a straight-line railway through winding mountain pass. Crash.

It is better to ask ourselves, "What if this or that fails or falls short?" The marketing program misfires, a product flops, a new competitor enters the market.

The answers provide a means to evaluate risk, attempt to avoid or minimize it, and to plan for recovery if it does happen. Or to abandon the plan and do something better.

A range of uncertainty

Harvard University and McKinsey & Company offered a four-tier method of planning under varying degrees of uncertainty:

Tier 1: Clear Enough Future (single view of the future)
Simple, because only one forecast is necessary and it is most likely to be accurate. Typical planning tools work, e.g., competitive analysis, market research, etc.

Most organizations in this tier are adapters. They decide where and how to best compete based upon well-known information.

Southwest Airlines, which has always been an innovative adapter, constantly refining their offerings to an established market.

Tier 2: Alternative Futures (set of possible future outcomes, one of which will occur)

The future is outlined as one of only a few possible outcomes, with some probabilities as to which one will. In any case, not all aspects of the strategy would have to change.

Often, those businesses that deal with legislative/regulatory changes fall into this level of uncertainty. Likewise, companies that cannot yet see competitor's expansion plans.

Witness the deregulation of phone companies and their plans to enter new markets. Until they could see the legislative timing, they had to guess at how they would expand.

Tier 3: Range of Futures (range of possible future outcomes)

Unlike Tier 2, there are no distinct outcome scenarios. Instead, there is a range of scenarios defined by a few key variables.

Those companies entering new geographies are in this Tier. E.g., if a new market penetration range is estimated at 10% to 30%, there is no distinct scenario within it.

As Mondex International and others used large investments to set standards for e-cash transactions, small banks had to invest internally for flexibility in adapting to outcomes.

Tier 4: Full Uncertainty (no range of potential future outcomes)

No certainty. While rare, it happens – and these companies will tend to migrate to one of the other Tiers in time. They may not even see relevant planning variables to use.

Companies who wanted to invest in post-communist Russia dealt with full uncertainty. They could predict virtually nothing at the time.

Netscape didn't rely on risky investment to shape Internet browser standards; they leveraged their credibility in the industry such that other players followed Netscape's lead.

The bottom lines

Uncertainty is certain. Learn how to do business planning with four levels of uncertainty: clear enough future, alternate futures, range of futures, and full uncertainty. Avoid unnecessary risk. Plan smart.

Leadership Lesson 19

Problems? Solve them with skill, support, and synchrony

Questions and answers. Q: what is a problem? A: an unwelcome situation needing to be overcome. Q: what is a solution? A: a means of dealing with a difficult circumstance. No secret that business problems emerge from any part of an organization. And beyond.

Problems from internal marketing, sales, engineering, and administration. Plus, external customers, vendors, and regulatory bodies. Endless.

"Leadership is solving problems. The day the team stops bringing you their problems is the day you have stopped leading them. They have either lost confidence that you can help or concluded you do not care. Either case is a failure of leadership." – *Colin Powell, former U.S. Secretary of State and retired Four-Star Army General*

Pay attention

Some problems are self-identifying. A quality assurance report says something is wrong with a product. Someone in engineering sees a design issue. Marketing and sales notes that a new promotion is not working as planned.

In other cases, someone outside the company identifies the problem. Customers complain about a product. A vendor notifies you that they cannot deliver to a timetable or a specification. Or the IRS has sent a love letter telling you that your company is being audited.

What doesn't work is to hide, avoid, or delay solving problems. What does work is to take action. Quickly.

Problem solving skills and behaviors

Learn how. Finding answers to obstacles is a logical step-process with the use of a strong, synchronous team:

- Clarifying the Problem – is it really a problem, is it the right problem, is it masking another problem?
- Organizing the Problem – get detailed facts, form a complete view of the organizations goals being affected and the impeding obstacles.
- Discovering the Possibilities – use a strong cross-functional team to brainstorm potential solutions, discuss and evaluate them.
- Making the Decision – analyze each solution for feasibility, costs, timing, risks and impacts to the organization; then decide which to implement.

- Implementing the Answer – select the people to implement the solution, set up milestones, and to launch and support the solutions team.
- Measuring the Progress – schedule regular meetings to track progress and to support the team; and to reward them when there has been a successful solution.

Effective problem also requires the leadership's caring support and collaborative results.

Don'ts and do's

Things to avoid include: blaming someone, criticism, being ignorant of costs, hit-and-miss or trial-and-error solutions, micromanaging the process, forcing a solution, acting disengaged, ignoring priorities. These things kill trust and teamwork.

Things to do are: listen a lot, be a mentor and coach, initially accept all ideas from the team, consolidate and discuss all ideas, us the group to prioritize ideas, get implementation ideas from the team. These are trust builders.

In the end, it is the leader's responsibility to make the final decision about which solution(s) will best resolve the problem in question. Good leadership in action.

Best benefits

There are a number of valuable returns, including: creative thinking, risk management, open communications, better solutions, stronger implementations, less bias, and faster results.

"We cannot solve our problems with the same thinking we used when we created them." – Einstein

The bottom lines

Skills. Behaviors. Both are part of the six-step process for effective problem solving. Use teams to find problems, prioritize them, create solutions, and implement them. It is the responsibility of good leaders for good business. Enjoy the many benefits.

Leadership Lesson 20

Missing anything? The one thing every leader must have

Endless. The ongoing lists of top characteristics, skills, and behaviors of the best business leaders don't stop. From books to blogs, research papers, and courses, leadership is described collectively as a business superpower. Yet the one must-have characteristic of top leaders is missing from these descriptions. And from too many leaders. What is it?

Call it "Mature Wisdom." No, not maturity and wisdom acquired in years. Maturity obtained by learning it. Wisdom by gained by learning it. Just as leaders learn to lead.

"Leaders are made, they are not born." – Vince Lombardi, former coach of the NFL Green Bay Packers football team

"Mature Wisdom" and outstanding leadership

When maturity (acting as an adult) and wisdom (having good judgment) are combined in a business leader, a powerful synergy is molded. The qualities of this enlightened leader create indelible visions, unstoppable teams, and successful, sustainable businesses. These leaders:

- Do not concern themselves with situations they cannot control.
- Listen carefully to the ideas of their teams and others.
- Handle unexpected, unpleasant events with composure.
- Accept responsibility for their decisions without alibis or blaming others.
- Act freely without emotional subservience to others.
- Follow the Golden Rule: treating others as they the leader want to be treated.
- Welcome constructive input gracefully and gratefully as a means to improve.
- Trust a Divine Providence as an ultimate guide for their lives.
- Are thoughtful and sensitive toward all others, equally.
- Take pleasure when others can accomplish things better than themselves.
- Can accept reasonable delays and can adapt to the needs of others.

And, they are flexible, knowing that they are not the mediator of the universe.

More …

Further, these "Mature Wisdom" leaders avoid persistent fault-finding with people, situations, and things. Additionally, they:

- Have a positive view of themselves and their feelings are not hurt easily.
- See infinite shades of gray, rather than black and white (or all or none).
- Stay away from self-pity, uncontrolled anger, or flashes of ego.
- Forgive quickly and release guilt, resentments, and envy.
- Are not ruled by their emotions and can make wise decisions as a result.
- Express honest happiness when others experience success – no jealousy.
- Endure losses without condemning anyone, including themselves.
- Plan things in advance, rather than making impulsive, moment-driven decisions.
- Gratefully helps others with no expectation of reward of any kind.
- Feel that they are part of humankind in total, giving their part to the whole.
- Mentor and teach their people the above skills and behaviors.

The point is that beyond all other good leadership qualities, including effective communications, relationship building, empowering others, successful delegation, visioning and planning – Mature Wisdom is the "secret sauce" of successful leadership.

And one more thing …

If the one thing leaders must have is "Mature Wisdom," the next thing they must have is "Authenticity." Having both is a magnetic attraction that engages other like-minded people. When we think, speak, and act from our authentic inner self we build trust – the not-so-secret-sauce of business success. Authenticity does not answer the question of "Who am I?" Authenticity affirms, "Who I am."

The bottom line

"Mature Wisdom." It is the one thing above all that all great leaders must have. And it is learned, not inbred. "Mature Wisdom" is a combined set of skills and behaviors that create unstoppable success. Add "Authenticity." Be a contagious leader.

Leadership Lesson 21

Drifting culture and adjusting the company's spine

Oh, sure. Strategic plan and the vision, purpose, mission, values. Very important, of course. Anybody mention "organizational culture?" In the annual overhaul of our annual plan, we re-evaluate our vision and mission. We spot new trends, market and competitive directions, and the business landscape. We are missing something. Culture.

Culture is the spinal column for the effective operation of the organization. Have a great vision, mission, and values – strong values embodied in the active attitudes and behaviors of the company is the real culture.

But there is a hidden flaw. What?

Oh, oh

We assume that even a great organizational and workplace culture once established is fixed forever. Bad assumption. Even if our vision, mission, and values have not changed, culture could have. Both the external and internal landscapes have moved.

Internally, there are new people, including leaders. Products and processes have been added, altered, and abandoned. Facilities have shifted.

Externally, markets are moving, competitors have joined in, and economies are different. The environment is changing.

Culture audit

Given that culture is the collective behaviors and attitudes of a group, where does it come from? The stated values of the company, the unstated values, and the values of leaders. Given the critical nature and impact of culture, why not review it annually? And here are some key questions to ask:

1. How do you describe the current culture in overall attitudes and behaviors?
2. How does is relate to the values of the organization?
3. Does the key leadership team of the company uphold this culture?
4. How is the culture any different than it was a year ago?
5. What internal and external influences caused it to change?
6. Were the changes negative, positive, or both?
7. Describe the gap between the existing culture and the desired one.
8. What impact is the existing culture having on the organization's performance?

---

9. What is missing from the culture?

10. Is there a cultural element that should be removed or altered?

11. What do we not know about our culture?

12. What would be our ideal culture and what has to change to get there?

Ask employees what they think of the culture. Also ask outsiders, such as customers and vendors. Gather up all the answers and ideas, and then assemble a small team to help define changes that are needed. And implement them.

A coffee culture

"When we began Starbucks, what I wanted to try to do was to create a set of values, guiding principles, and culture." – Howard Schultz, executive chairman

The primary components of Starbucks organizational culture are:

- Servant Leadership ("employees first")
- Relationship-driven approach
- Collaboration and communication
- Openness
- Inclusion and diversity

Panmore Institute defines Starbucks's organizational culture as a highly distinct feature. While seen in the corporate offices, this culture is easily observed in the 25,000 cafes worldwide – how the employees interact with each other and with customers. The friendly, inviting ambiance is a clear distinction from most competitors. Their culture relates to the successful strategy for brand development and global expansion. A strong serving.

The bottom lines

Culture. Understand it, its powerful impact, and its relationship to your vision, mission and values. Know what goes into it. Importantly, do not take it for granted. Review it annually and keep it relevant. Internally and externally.

Leadership Lesson 22

From slow to fast with a bias toward action

Talkers. Evaluators. Postulators. Everything but getting something important done. When an organization spends excessive time "getting ready to get ready to act," there is too little focus on absolute action. Why?

Too often the leader does not have a strong bias toward action. If so, the organization will tend to follow. If the reality of results falls short of planned goals, the question is why? Little sense of urgency, low expectations. Weak sense of responsibility and accountability. S-l-o-w.

Contrast: Amazon's leadership principle #8 is "A Bias for Action." 5th largest U.S. corporation by market capitalization, 12th largest by revenues. F-a-s-t.

What holds us back?

Some form of fear is often the leash that stalls stepping into action. Psychologists have provided several reasons for why we stay stopped rather than start starting:

1. *Fear of failure* - some of us don't act because we do not want to be blamed for something that does not work out as expected.

2. *Fear of success* - if we feel unworthy or undeserving, then staying behind is safer than being recognized as a hero.

3. *Fear of uncertainty* - if we cannot be certain of what will happen, we will not run the risk of beginning.

4. *Fear of change* - oh yes, "we don't know how to do this," or "we have never done this before," or "it won't make any difference" - ergo, it is safer to stay put.

5. *Fear of imperfection* - if we lack some small resource, we continuously play out the game of "not ready yet," but the competitive clock is running.

These anesthetizing anxieties close the portals of possibilities and extinguish the excitement of achieving success.

Jump starts

It seems simple. And it is. Decide what to do and why, who will do it, when, and where. The implementation team can figure out how. Give the team resources and leadership support, establish milestones of progress, and set up periodic progress reviews. Paradox: it takes action to put ideas into action.

Leadership support is critical. The leader can provide positive moral support, needed resources, and mentoring and coaching.

If the team senses that it is not there, the team will fall back, disengage, and action will stall. This is leadership failure.

Likewise, collaborative results are important. The leader must form an engaged team, help them work together closely, and foster the delivery of a team-based solution. If potential solutions become the "property" of individuals rather than the team as a whole, there is no real team. Again, leadership has failed.

False starts

Jumping into action before there is a reasonable plan upon which to act results in scattered effort – with weak or no results. Likewise, waiting for excessive data in order to start is within "the law of diminishing returns." General Colin Powell was satisfied enough with 50% to 70% of the data he needed for a decision to act.

When there is one foot on the accelerator, and the other foot on the brake, things go nowhere. The team is not united.

"Do not mistake motion for action." – Ernest Hemmingway, American author

The bottom lines

Go! Develop a strong bias toward action. Don't wait. Assemble teams, form action plans, assign roles and responsibilities, track progress, reward success. Simple. Most of all, as a leader offer real support and foster collaborative results. Do it now.

Leadership Lesson 23

5 ways to puncture stagnation and innovate innovation

Nothing new. Your company has few if any new products. Yet competition is on a creative binge. This is the path to terminal stagnation. You can wait until someone in the organization comes up with the next winning idea. Dangerous. Or, you can build an intensely innovative culture. In other words, innovate innovation. How?

There is no right time to be creative. Be creative constantly. It is the way of a successful business life. Develop a creative culture that spins out a bright stream of highly innovative ideas. Particularly those that are contrarian.

"I have always been driven to buck the system, to innovate, to take things beyond where they've been." – Sam Walton, founder of Walmart

Counter-culture

Be prepared for people to call you crazy when you introduce highly novel, Igottahaveit products. Contrarian stuff. Who would buy books (and everything else) on the Internet? Who would want an electric car? Who would want a computer on their desk – or in their briefcase?

Extreme innovation produces products that change the world. And build entire new corporations and industries. Not just "high tech" – but things like 3M Sticky Notes, microbreweries, meals in a box to cook at home, inexpensive Lyft transportation. Endless.

How do these things happen? Read on.

Innovating innovation

So how do we and our organizations become more innovative? Here are five ways to do it:

1. Get information – purchase research reports for your industry, use "big data" resources to understand your market, ask customers what else they want, listen to customer complaints and solve them. Heinz saw their catsup customers turning bottles upside down – so Heinz designed upside-down bottles.

2. Motivate the organization – ask employees to bring new ideas forward), hold offsite innovation retreats, have periodic brainstorming sessions, add innovation to everyone's objectives, incent developers – 3M pays their

engineers to innovate, largely based upon the success of their innovative Post-It Notes.

3. Go outside – use social media to survey, collaborate with another company, work with an innovative university to develop new products, hold an outside contest for innovative ideas, license someone else's patents and incorporate them – Dolby sound technology has been imbedded in audio equipment for decades.

4. Think without boundaries – ask "what if" questions, solve contradictory conditions (e.g., make a faster product while using less power), retro a former product (e.g., the VW Bug), eliminate an industry standard (Amazon did it to bookstores), combine separate products – Ericson's first camera in a phone.

5. Build an innovation culture – hire an Innovation Officer to drive creativity, make innovation an organizational value, innovate internally with advanced processes and systems, update the logo to make it look innovative, establish an innovation lab – done by Lockheed in their Skunkworks to create exotic "it cannot be done" aircraft.

Ford Motor Company developed a new innovation culture in 2006, turned the company around financially, and was the only U.S. automotive producer who did not need federal government "bailout money" in the 2008 financial crisis. Point made.

The bottom lines

Innovation. It is the soul of successful businesses. Learn more about how to better innovate – ergo, innovating innovation. It is an art and a science. Build a list of actions to take in building a culture of innovation. Promote and reward innovation. Do it all the time. You can change your company, your industry, and the world. Ask Amazon.

Leadership Lesson 24

What is the unfinished business of business?

Incomplete. Something missing from the overall picture of your company. An out of date business plan. A process that is not working. A product line that is stagnate. Oh, and some staffing that is no longer adequate. Fact: there is unfinished business throughout the business. But where is it?

That is the question to ask the team: where is our most important unfinished business? Perhaps it is something that can be completed. OK, by whom and when? Or, if it cannot be finished, or is not worth it, then drop it. Pivot and move a new direction.

Who needs to deal with this condition? The leader, of course.

The quest

Ask a good team member to take on the task of locating all unfinished business in the organization. Build the list, ask your team to help prioritize and evaluate it, and decide what to finish, what to stop, and what to put on a back burner for a while.

There are numerous sources of unfinished business. Every department of the organization, input from customers and prospects, talking to vendors. Where is our unfinished business?

This should be the full-time business of one, trusted person – sometimes the leader. If this not happening in some way, then this alone is critical unfinished business. Paradox!

The blockages

Here are some real reasons that we don't deal with unfinished business:

- Sometimes we are so engrossed in doing new things that we fail to finish prior things.
- Our people are not well trained in the art and science of follow-up.
- Some employees will subconsciously drag things out just to keep their job.
- We are aware of some unfinished business, but we ignore it out of laziness.
- Or, "It is somebody else's job, not mine."
- Believe it or not, fear of success will prevent some people from completing things.
- Finishing older tasks may not carry enough reward and recognition.

- Someone is promoted or leaves, and their incomplete task is not delegated to another.

- The potentially high cost (and waste) of incomplete work is not understood.

- More simply, the leader is not leading. Really.

Too many of us are not aware of The Power of Completion.

Alt view

Yes, there are some rational reasons to support some appropriate level of unfinished work. One of these is that if everything is always done, we can lack a sense of purposefulness and excitement.

Completing unfinished business can be an opportunity to solve problems via good teamwork. And, the people who complete the unfinished work can be rewarded and feel good about what they have accomplished.

The famous "Unfinished Symphony" by composer Franz Schubert was actually declared as finished on a technicality by another composer after Schubert's death. This music is considered as a classical success.

A relay of success

Sometimes, unfinished work can be left for others who have new skills and energies to advance the completion. Steve Jobs left plenty of unfinished business for his successor at Apple, Tim Cook – who has run the next lap of the Apple "relay of success."

The bottom lines

Unfinished. What are the unfinished assignments in your organization – and what is the cost? Find an "Unfinished Business Guru" in your organization. Finish that which really needs completion, and let the rest go. Save time, save money. Reward completion.

Leadership Lesson 25

The naked truth about cash flow

Stripped. In the shower of various financial statements what do we normally receive? Income Statement (aka, Profit & Loss Statement – P&L), check. Balance Sheet, check. Cash Flow Statement, check. Various ratio analyses, check. Ooooops, something missing. What?

Hello, Cash Flow Projection. In a given month, the common cash flow statement tells us how much cash we took in, how much cash went out, and how much cash we ended with. Problem: we do not have a clean view of how much estimated cash we will need over the next several months. Dangerous blind spot. What to do?

"We've demonstrated a strong track record of being very disciplined with the use of our cash. We don't let it burn a hole in our pocket, we don't allow it to motivate us to do stupid acquisitions. We feel that there are one or more strategic opportunities in the future." – Steve Jobs, co-founder and former CEO of Apple

Thought shift

Most entrepreneurs believe that getting to break-even revenue and expenses is the holy grail. The holier grail is to get to positive cash flow and stay there. Warning: do not depend upon income statements and balance sheets to portray real cash flow. Why not?

> *An income statement can mask accurate liquid cash. E.g., recording increased sales (orders) that include special deals and discounts. This can raise the cost of sales and lower net cash revenues (income).*

> *A balance sheet can disfigure a true cash position if excessive cash is tied up in inventories and accounts receivables. Inventories must to be sold to become accounts receivables, and receivables must be collected for the actual cash to exist.*

A solid cash flow statement will normalize these and other distortions and provide a good understand of past and current cash positions.

Fortune telling

Now turn to future cash flow needs and stop running blind. What will our real cash flow look like going forward? How much cash will we need to operate and grow the business? And when will we need it? Ask your CFO to generate a formal monthly Cash Flow Projection.

Downside: we do not want to be caught without enough cash to run the business. No cash to meet payroll? Ugly surprise.

Upside: Strong cash generation and management provide:

- Growth – a company may need to invest in technology, equipment and facilities - and sometimes acquire other companies or pay dividends.

- Survival – we are better able to survive economic downturns by having adequate cash.

- Emergency – a better handle on unexpected expenses that need to be paid.

- Frugality – keep expenses low by paying cash in appropriate instances; e.g., reduce transaction and bank fees.

- Buffer – avoid the need for expensive, short-term loans.

"Cash is king. Get every drop of cash you can get and hold onto it." – Jack Welch, former CEO of General Electric

Biggest piggy banks

Reported by *Business Insider* in December 2017, the largest U.S. corporate holders of cash are:

1. Apple $262B
2. Microsoft $133B
3. Alphabet (Google) $95B
4. Cisco $68B
5. Oracle $66B

A cash-healthy club - just look at their stock prices.

The bottom lines

Cash. The fuel of business growth. Not just cash on hand, or past cash usage – but the projected cash flow over the next many months is essential. Ask your CFO to give you a future Cash Flow Projection. Now.

Leadership Lesson 26

The toxic temptations of a lazy leader

Slippage. "Down is faster than up" often refers to the stock market. But it applies well to individual businesses. The admonishment to not take our eyes off the road when driving is true of a rapidly moving business environment. Example?

Kodak. It took 100 years to build a great global company. But in the late 1990's the "Kodak Moment" failed – and quickly. By 2012, Kodak was bankrupt. Why? They continued to focus on film-based photography and ignored the silent storm of digital images. Snap.

"The temptation of business is always to feed yesterday and to starve tomorrow." – Peter Drucker, management guru, writer, university professor

Seductions, allures, and fascinations

Here are some popular temptations that weak or unobservant leaders too often fall to recognize. Giving in to any one of these evils can ruin a good business. And succumbing to several of them simultaneously will kill the business. Quickly.

Disregard loose reins

Those things that created a good business are being ignored. Purpose, vision, mission, values, strategy, execution. The leader needs to wake up, reboot the business, strengthen it, and accelerate to sustainable success.

Ho-hum apathy

The stealthy companions of complacently include declining passion, increasing apathy, and the strangle-hold of "we don't have any competition" are big holes into hades. Real leaders should set the action-alarm and awaken the company with new, positive energy.

Tune out teams

Poor hiring practices plus retaining under-performing employees for too long takes the luster off a once-gleaming organization. Leaders must replace deadwood with excellent people. Continuously train the team and reward good performers. Visibly.

Ignore stale stuff

Old products and services are no longer attractive in the market. Little innovation and creativity throughout the organization – marketing, sales, and customer service included. A good leader will stir innovation into the culture and ignite creativity.

Look past dirty dashboards

Few standards and no controls. The critical information that the organization needs to operate efficiently either does not exist, or is invisible. Leader: set standards, put financial and other controls in place, track, and report. Celebrate when goals are met.

Fail to see torn roadmaps

The market is shifting, the customer base is changing, and marketing is oblivious. Competition is unleashing new products. Astute leaders will get internal and external accurate market data – and then respond with new products and marketing programs.

Brush off care-less customer care

Sloppy service and little respect for customers. The organization does not care. Leaders insist that sales, service, and everyone develop and implement deep-care programs for customers. It costs much less to keep a customer than to find a new one.

Neglect critical cash reports

Loans, investors, cash flow are not sustaining nor accelerating growth of the business. A solid leader will form plans to generate generous amounts of cash. This leader will pursue cash well before it is needed – and have a lot of cash in reserve.

Worse yet, a deadly, dogmatic attachment to whatever has worked in the past is deemed good enough for now – ignoring the fact that change is constant. Hold to the vision, not the past.

The bottom lines

Beware. Be aware of the toxic temptations that bombard off-guard business leaders. Loose standards, apathy, stagnation, poor information, worn out dogma. And more. Wake up, plug in, and reenergize a still-living business. Before it is too late.

Leadership Lesson 27

Dirty dancing with business transactions before building business relationships?

Backward. Trying to conduct business transactions before building any kind of customer relationship? Doable, but not durable. One good conversation can begin the creation of a two-way relationship that has meaning, trust, and persistence. Hello?

Don't begin a business transaction until something other than a phone connection has been made. A real connection is less brain-based, and more soul-based. An authentic, interpersonal association will open doors. The discovery of common ground works wonders – where we have lived or visited, someone we know, a movie we love, or a food we enjoy. A relationship has begun.

When you dance, your purpose is not to get to a certain place on the floor. It's to enjoy each step along the way. – Wayne Dyer, psychologist, author, speaker

Relationships, transactions, and partnerships

Here's the idea. As leaders, we want long term business relationships with our customers and clients. At every level. Our great marketing, sales, customer service, accounting, and other customer interfaces are built upon solid trust. Authenticity.

Sure, you can get an order in short order with a direct hit in a fast sale. If that customer senses that all your sales person wants is the order, this might be the only business from that buyer.

Why not take a little more time to build a relationship with that same customer – it could bring years of a buyer-vendor partnership that serves both well. Very well.

The business of communications

Here are some proven ways to communicate effectively and build effective business relationships with customers (or anyone else):

<u>Two-way</u> – every solid conversation must be bi-directional, not just one-way. Keep the dialog going and make it more interesting by true interaction with the customer or prospect. Understand what they are saying, and be understood by them.

<u>Ask questions</u> – this is a powerful way to engage the customer, particularly a new customer. From a relationship-building view,

simply ask the client, "Where were you born and raised," and then tell them your birthplace. This can build a connection.

<u>Stay focused</u> – once the conversation starts to flow, stay with it. When it is time to ask the customer how you can best help them, their response is critical and requires even more focus. Your response can strengthen the bond of trust for both of you.

<u>Humor helps</u> – a little lightheartedness usually helps relax the conversation. It puts people at ease, builds the relationship, and can make the business part of the interchange go more smoothly. Particularly self-deprecating humor about ourselves.

<u>Listen more</u> – talk less. Harvard University recommends sales people listen ten times more than talk. Easy – we listen at 300 words per minute and speak at 100 words per minute. A relationship builder. And, this is how we really learn what our client wants.

These are only a few techniques for creating conversations effectively, and building strong relationships with customer. The subsequent sales transactions will flow more freely. And frequently.

Apple, Amazon, and action

Deep dialogs with customers have another big benefit. Companies like Apple and Amazon interact obsessively with their customers to understand market trends, to be more customer-focused, and to turn customer feedback into positive actions. Success.

The bottom lines

Talk first. Build relationships second. Enjoy business transactions third. Interactive conversations with customers build the kind of durable relationships and partnerships that create better business. For the customer. And for good leaders and their teams. Always.

Leadership Lesson 28

Lost your business "voice?" Find it here

Laryngitis? No, the "little voice within." Dictionary: "the supposed utterance of a guiding spirit giving instructions or advice." Your professional purpose. The "why" of your company or organization. Your values and culture. But how did you lose this inner voice?

You followed other people's opinions, instead of your own. Or you were pushed by your ego. Consequently, your own inner voice was muffled. Or muzzled. You could no longer hear it.

Don't let the noise of others' opinions drown out your own inner voice. And most important, have the courage to follow your heart and intuition. – Steve Jobs, co-founder and former CEO of Apple, Inc.

Spin out

Leaders can succumb to significant pressures – too often of the wrong kind. Former H-P CEO Mark Hurd submitted phony expense reports covering his relationship with a contractor.

The CEO of Lehman Brothers, Richard Fuld, kept denying that the firm did not have enough capital. And rejected advice repeatedly to find more. When the Great Recession rolled in it killed Lehman and rattled the entire global financial system. Bailout time.

Energy giant Enron employed 20,000 people and had stated revenues of $100 billion by year 2000. But Enron died of a rapid bankruptcy brought on by a systemic, systematic reporting of fraudulent financial information. Dead by year 2004.

Shout out

Take time to rediscover the voice that has served you well. Or, find a newer voice that can move you forward. Reset the tone of the real you – not someone else's "you."

1. Understand your innermost values and beliefs. Write them, examine them, and ask others who know you well to give you feedback. Do others see you as you see yourself?

2. Are you living your values in your professional (and personal) life – including when there are pressures and conflicts. Great leaders always to the right thing – no matter what.

3. Ask your inner voice to help you understand how to bring it back stronger than ever. Even though quieted for long, our inner knowing is always ready to respond.

4. Always assume that there is more than you can see. Time spent in the silence, in meditation, will help you rediscover (or discover) your true values and voice.

5. Persist in this treasure hunt to have your own true voice, authentic, unbending, purposeful. Any less than this robs you of your highest leadership skills and behaviors.

6. Manage stress because the more stressed we are, the fainter our voice of wisdom, our inner voice, becomes. Exercise, meditation, stress management seminars. All good.

7. Patience is not only a virtue – it is key to upping the volume of our inner voice. Being stressed about how we are doing in finding our wisdom-inside is self-defeating.

Everyone who wills can hear their inner voice. It is within everyone. – Mahatma Gandhi, Indian non-violent activist

Stand out

Starbucks CEO, Howard Schultz, founded the company the same year his father died from long-term health issues. A few years later, Starbucks became the first U.S. company to offer health care for all of its employees. Inner voice, outer purpose.

The bottom lines

Find your voice. Your inner voice of wisdom. It is the quiet expression of your values, expressed as the culture of your organization. It is a compass that points to the true-north of your success as a leader. Authenticity.

Leadership Lesson 29

Too slow? Run everything like a startup

Alarm. As we awaken with coffee, start our day, get into our office, we have an amazing opportunity. We can look at today as a continuation of yesterday – or we can do a daily startup. Like a startup business, what are the high priorities right now? Launch the day.

And, we can run our business, giant or small, as a startup. Lean, hungry, quick, striving, focused – utilizing all aspects of great leadership. Too big? Look at Amazon – lean, mean, and green. Too small? look at starburst startups like Zoom Video Communications. Founded 2011, 40 million participants and 65,000 organizational subscribers by 2015. Zoom.

Learning to see waste and systematically eliminate it has allowed lean companies such as Toyota to dominate entire industries. Lean thinking defines value as "providing benefit to the customer"; anything else is waste. Eric Ries, American businessman, author of "The Lean Startup"

The startup mind

So, what are the critical skills and behaviors of startup leaders that can be applied to running both larger and smaller businesses?

- Run lean – continuously eliminate all unnecessary resources; programs, processes, people.
- Run fast – move swiftly in every area of the business with a bias toward action.
- Run differently – don't copy competition; take the lead with unique products and markets.
- Run creatively – innovate constantly with people, products, processes, services.
- Run purposefully – define the outer reason for the business; do something good for humanity.
- Run organized – always do the most important things first; re-prioritize every morning.
- Run generously – be giving to employees, customers, others; develop lasting teams.
- Run clearly – hold to a stated, communicated vision all along the way.
- Run authentically – be completely honest with yourself and others; build trust.
- Run deeply – dig into details and expect your teams to do the same.
- Run broadly – understand markets, trends and (especially) what customers want.
- Run welcoming – invite creative ideas from everyone for products and processes, and for solutions to problems.

- Run together – invite outside companies and resources to collaborate.
- Run optimally – every day, make the best possible use of resources; find the focal points for action.
- Run flexibly – quickly pivot away from things that do not work, and toward those that can or do work; and allow failures.
- Run communicatively – keep employees, customers, prospects, communities and others informed, honestly (don't hide bad news.
- Run positively – keeping an affirmative view helps the entire organization be buoyant, especially during challenging events.
- Run gratefully – genuinely thank employees, customers, suppliers, others who deserve your appreciation.

Above all, run accurately. Speed matters, unless it makes a mess. So, run fast and stay between the lines of excellence. And clean up any messes.

Entrepreneurial culture

Build a value system that supports an entrepreneurial culture. In any size organization. In a large organization it is often called, "intrapreneurial."

And it is not just about hot tech products. It is about everything. The people, the processes, the products. In every segment of the business: marketing, sales, customer service, IT, engineering, production, administration. Everything.

Especially leadership.
132

The bottom lines

Lean. Fast. Flexible. Three of many entrepreneurial skills and behaviors. But not unique to startup companies. They are equally valuable in large companies. Amazon gets it. Kodak didn't. Plant the culture of startup companies in any organization. It begins with the leader, continues to sustainable success, and never ends. Ever.

Leadership Lesson 30

Boxed in thinking? Get out of it now

The boxes. Ways of thinking and leading. Typically, we think that we are either "in the box" (conventional thinking) or "out of the box" (unconventional thinking). We are ignoring the fact that there are more boxes. Really?

Paradox. We are already "in the box" when we believe that there are only those two possibilities: in-the-box or out-of-the-box. And, we hold that being out-of-the-box as the only way to think, and being in-the-box is restrictive.

Not true.

More Boxes ...

What if there at least two more variations of "the box?" (oh, by the way, no box is better or worse than another box – all are needed, appropriately):

- In the box.
- Straddle the box.

- Out of the box.
- No box.

So, what's the application in our real business world? Here are some broad characteristics and examples for our four "boxed" ways of thinking.

"In the Box" – Conventional ways of getting things done

- More rules: solid guidelines about work content.
- Little creativity: there is no room for other possibilities.
- Focused motivation: people are urged to work specifically.
- Specific action: time lines and fixed quantities of work must be met.

Examples of industries and jobs that have a high level of in-the-box thinking:

Manufacturing production

Public administration

Transportation systems

Organizations that excel with an in-the-box culture encompass IBM, fire departments, highway departments, and UPS.

"Straddle the Box" – Standard ways of doing things, but with flexibility

- Some rules: work is done within guidelines, with some variations.
- More creativity: encouragement to see new refinements in processes.
- More motivation: room to express ideas for improved products.
- Flexible action: latitude for different actions based upon circumstances.

Examples of industries and jobs that tend to made good use of this style include:

> *Hospitality*
> *Retail sales*
> *Banking/Financial*

Businesses good at standardized approaches to their operations, yet are noted for some elasticity in dealing with customers, include Hyatt, Wendy's, Nordstrom's, and Citibank.

"Out of the Box" – Unconventional ways of thinking

- Few rules: the environment is largely unrestricted for most work.
- High creativity: ideas flow freely and are examined for possible use.
- Strong motivation: ideas for continuous improvement are expressed.
- Rapid action: good ideas move quickly into reality quickly.

Example jobs and industries that tend to be more out-of-the-box:

Technology

Retail

Marketing

Some companies that have demonstrated out-of-the-box thinking include Apple, Amazon, Tesla, and Southwest Airlines.

"No Box" – No Precedents, no rules

- No rules: more spontaneity in an open environment with naturally formed teams.
- Maximum creativity: a constant stream of great visions, ideas and possibilities.
- High motivation: people work with an unseen energy that is often amazing.
- Synchronous action: things happen with stunning speed.

Examples of no-box activities are:

Pure research

Brainstorming sessions

Creating or solving "the impossible"

Entities that exhibited no-box thinking include Xerox and xerography, Intel and semiconductors, Lockheed's SR-71 aircraft, and the U.S. successful race to the moon.

No one size fits all

Good leaders avoid conforming to just one kind of box. They intelligently and intentionally move among all the boxes dynamically as needed. E.g., different departments need different ways of operating. The best leaders find the right boxes for each.

The bottom lines

Understand which box styles your leadership operates. Discover how alternative box types would help the organization. Take a step toward adopting a new or added box style that can boost the business. In-the-box, straddle-the-box, out-of-the-box, or no-box.

Leadership Lesson 31

6 steps to remove a rotten apple from the barrel

Toxicity. One employee is increasingly anti. Anti-culture, anti-policy, anti-business plan, and anti-you. Problem: they are poisoning other employees. And they affect productivity, turnover, and the business. What to do?

Adage: "One rotten apple will spoil the rest of the barrel." If they are affecting other good employees and the overall business is suffering, then why keep them? You could be dealing with a prima donna and afraid to let them go. Or, you are turning your head.

Even if the bad employee has an important skill, they are causing unwarranted and unwanted damage. Why wait to remove them? Replace them.

"No bad apples in my organization"

Bet? Remember these unnerving statistics, per Gallup research:

- 51% of employees are not engaged (potential bad apples)
- 17% are actively creating trouble (bad apples)
- 32% of employees are engaged (good apples)

However, from a GloboForce white paper, "The Science of Happiness," happy employees are:

- 58% more likely to help a customer or a colleague
- 98% more likely to identify with company values and goals
- 186% more likely to recommend their company for employment and for business

And in a study by the "iOpener Institute for People and Performance," engaged, enthusiastic employees:

- Are twice as productive
- Stay five times longer in their jobs
- Take 10 times less sick leave

Now that you are convinced to remove the negative employees, how do you do it?

Purging the barrel

Here are 6 steps to remove bad employees from your organization:

1. Find them – you might already know who some of the unengaged and disengaged employees are. But if you are ducking the issue, consider the damage being done – and consider the benefits of removing these people. Reality.

2. Be careful – if you have good, but unengaged, people in your organization, why? If the leadership team is not engaging otherwise good employees, look first to leadership. Or lack of it.

3. See HR – follow their directions for identifying and documenting the "for cause" reasons to remove the bad apples. Perhaps they need to be warned first, and given an opportunity to improve. Or not.

4. Let go – systematically remove the offenders, fairly and following HR guidelines. Perhaps those let go will find better opportunities with other employers. And, it is likely that other better employees will be happy to see them leave. And be more engaged.

5. Hire others – there is a good chance that you will not miss the people you remove in terms of the workload. They are likely not performing well. If you do need to promote or hire people to replace them, you can find far better employees. Improvement.

6. Communicate it – not as a warning, but as a positive way to let the organization know that the leaders are leading. And that there is no tolerance for negative people. That the management team does care about the good employees. A lot.

Remember that 15%+ of your organization could be bad apples – and that happy, engaged employees are twice as productive.

The bottom lines

Remove toxic employees. They are poisoning those around them. 17% of U.S. workers are disengaged and causing problems. Morale, productivity, profitability. Find the disengaged and remove them. The other employees will benefit. So will the business. So will you.

Leadership Lesson 32

How to avoid the dangerous dance of a maddening unleader

Unleader? Yes, a pseudo-leader who unravels employees, customers, and others. All in a tight and tense environment. Short-term performance at all costs, including the loss of good employees. A widening view of control – until there is nothing left to control.

Once you understand that you are an unleader, either transform yourself to a true leader, or continue to squeeze the life out of your organization. If you are working for an unleader and miserable, leave. Fire yourself and find an uplifting organization. Soon.

Gallup surveys continue to note that over 50% of U.S. employees are disengaged, 17% are actively making trouble, and 34% are engaged. And happy.

Understanding the unleader

Read the following list and decide if you are an unleader, working for one, or are unclear. Even a few of these characteristics can create a toxic culture:

- Unleaders must know where employees are and what they are doing, always.
- Unleaders believe that they can do every job better than their employees.
- Unleaders push all blame for everything to the employees.
- Unleaders are feared by their employees.
- Unleaders cause their employees to feel depressed.
- Unleaders over-assert their authority.
- Unleaders are controlled by their stress.
- Unleaders don't know their numbers or value what their employees are creating.
- Unleaders impose very task-oriented roles for employees.
- Unleaders provide training that is rigid about how things must be done.
- Unleaders are reluctant about delegating tasks to employees.
- Unleaders see vulnerability as a weakness.
- Unleaders dictate how a task is to be done.
- Unleaders view their employees as robots to make money.
- Unleaders are not leaders – they are poor managers at best.

These are the reasons why employees are disengaged, turnover is high, and productivity is low. Time to make a turn.

Learn about the leader

Real leaders serve and preserve their employees. Knowing that great employees build great customers. How do these leaders do it. Much easier than being an unleader:

- Leaders lift and excite their employees.
- Leaders celebrate wins by acknowledging individuals and teams, regularly.
- Leaders encourage their employees to identify problems and help solve them.
- Leaders accept accountability for their own failures and don't blame employees.
- Leaders describe clearly what they want their people to produce.
- Leaders will negotiate milestone dates with what is to be delivered and when.
- Leaders will see vulnerability as a real strength for themselves and employees.
- Leaders manage stress well for themselves and their teams.
- Leaders delegate effectively with clarity and mutual commitment.
- Leaders provide regular performance reviews with their employees.
- Leaders review programs and projects for progress, helping the teams improve.
- Leaders are approachable by their people.
- Leaders do not play favorites.
- Leaders mentor, coach, teach and promote their people.

- Leaders value employees for their creativity and problem-solving skills.

These are the leaders that develop engaged and happy employees.

Benefits beyond …

Gallup research also finds that engaged employees provide:

- 22% better profitability.
- 21% more productivity.
- 37% less absenteeism.

Outstanding leaders go out of their way to boost the self-esteem of their personnel. If people believe in themselves, it's amazing what they can accomplish. – Sam Walton, Walmart founder

The bottom lines

Undo unleadership. Be a real leader. Stamp out toxic cultures and create empowering work environments. Develop engaged employees. Benefit from more productivity, less disengagement, and greater profitability. Be happy.

Leadership Lesson 33

Workplace gloom and 7 steps to stop it

Gray? If your work environment has an drab emotional pall over it, look around. Oh, and start with the mirror. If you are a leader, manager, supervisor, or individual contributor, how are you contributing to this spirit-stomping darkness?

When is the last time you experienced something funny at work, and laughed without restraint? *Psychology Today* notes that our brain cannot process fear and a laughter, simultaneously. Let us train ourselves to "laugh it off."

Oh, and there are real benefits to appropriate humor in the workplace. It neutralizes fear, relaxes and settles us down, reduces pain, and raises our spirits. Try it.

Business leaders lighten up

Forbes Magazine wrote, "Tasteful humor is a key to success at work, but there's a good chance your co-workers aren't cracking jokes or packaging information with wit on a regular basis—and your office could probably stand to have a little more fun."

For more than 25 years, we have loved the daily cartoons by Scott Adams, *Dilbert*. We giggle and howl about the unwitting, nutty, (and too often true) attitudes of people at work. All of us. Including leaders.

More benefits: humor improves productivity, promotes creativity, expands learning, builds teamwork. It builds better leadership skills and behaviors. Spread some appropriate fun each day with other employees, vendors, and customers.

Fly fun

Southwest Airlines founder, Herb Kelleher, created a company culture loved by his employees. He was the "clown prince" of the airlines, often in costume. His employees followed by singing their humorous announcements to passengers – yet serious about doing their jobs well.

The company has been among the most admired American corporations, and Kelleher one of the best CEOs, in *Fortune Magazine's* annual poll—lauding the airline's upbeat service. Herb unscored servant leadership, wherein happy employees foster happy customers. Repeat customers.

The bond between Kelleher and his employees helped provide Southwest over 23 consecutive years of profitability.

Laws of laughter at work

1. Add some fun to your workplace and odds are that if you are having a good time, others will, too. Laughter is contagious and they will follow you.
2. Self-deprecating humor, poking fun at yourself highlights your authenticity as a human, and others will see it. And, they might add a some more laughter by revealing their own humorous.
3. A sense of lightness can be versatile enough to improve most situations. Create more enjoyment of work by adding a shot of laughter each day.
4. Be professional. Don't demean others or embarrass them. Use appropriate, clean humor. Fun can help just about everyone and does not always have to cause laughter – big smiles are good, too.
5. Encourage other people to use humor. Support them by smiling and laughing to let them know you appreciate their fun side.
6. Choose events within the organization (or outside) just to have fun. Get together for a light hearted meal. Or, everyone go to a laugh-driven movie and eat afterward.
7. Don't overdo it. The organization's business is serious and needs to be treated accordingly. People can enjoy some humor and continue to be great employees.

The bottom lines

Lighten up. And light up your organization. Laugh at yourself and encourage humor by others. Be appropriate about using humor and others will follow. See the organization become more creative, productive, and healthier in mind, body and spirit. Smile!

Leadership Lesson 34

Hell in the hallway of creative change – handle it

You've heard it. "When one door closes, another one opens." What the originators and purveyors of this adage did not tell us is that the hallway between the two is dark and hot with fear. Can't turn back. What happened?

We lost a job, missed a great opportunity, or a key customer left us. All doors seemingly closed, no guiding lights, and accelerating angst. Cornered.

Or so it seems. What to do while burning down the hallway – toward the next door of opportunity?

Hallway Instructions

Here are some long-tested ways to move through this passage of change with minimum gasping and maximum grace:

Do not panic – it only makes things worse. Instead, relax and realize that this is a moment of change, a chance for creative change. Something good is gestating. Relax.

See opportunity – while the next door opening has not occurred, what would you like to see behind it? Envision it and hold on. The likelihood is that it will happen – even bigger.

No forcing it – don't shove the door to a new possibility. Instead, allow Divine Providence to open up a perfect door from the field of all possibilities – just for you.

Take a break – this moment of shift will move more miraculously if we take our mind off it. Spend a few days to unwind, learn from the experience, be ready for a bigger door.

Test it – when you start to see some light under the next door of a greater moment, find out more about it. Is it a false alarm – or a solid possibility for you?

Communicate – talk about the situation with others you trust. Family members, friends, other work associates, mentors, and counselors. No need to be alone – get support.

Journal – many who make the passage of change keep a daily log of feelings, thoughts, ideas, dreams and desires. This fosters a more rational receptivity to new opportunities.

Practice patience –we want the process to happen quickly, but that is not always the way with change. As we keep moving through the passage, the next door will open.

"Let it be" – Beatles' John Lennon sang it, and it reminds us that the seeds of creative change have been sown. Now, it is time to allow the field of all possibilities to ripen.

Act on it – the new door finally opens and a new possibility appears. Be grateful for it, evaluate it, and if it resonates with your desires, take action to capture this opportunity.

The above guides will help you walk the hallway's hot coals of change with more comfort and receptivity for an exciting, creative change.

Henry and the new door

Henry Ford declared bankruptcy in 1903. The door closed. After more failures, he walked the dark hallway, a new door opened, and Henry saw the reality of his dream emerge in the Ford Motor Company. His estimated net worth today would be $188 billion. And, his products serve millions of people globally.

The bottom lines

Slam. A current door just closed and you lost something important. Such as a job. No going back. And you want a new, better door of opportunity to open. First, walk the dark hallway between the two doors. Follow the above Hallway Instructions for an easier walk. To your next success.

Leadership Lesson 35

Something big changed. Now how do you communicate it?

Different. Something in the business has changed, is changing, or is likely to change. What is it, where is it, and how important is it? Given its impact on the business, what will you do about it? Read on.

Communicating the change to others appropriately is a good first move. Who needs to know, how do you tell them, and what is expected of them? Change without sufficient communications causes doubt, and the rumor mills grind out the debris of distrust.

Change is the only constant in life. – Heraclitus, Greek philosopher

What moved?

A change already happened. We hear about it from someone. We ask about changes from our organizations and we find out. And, our financial reports tell us. Sometimes in harsh ways.

A change is already occurring? Make it easy for others to let us know, and encourage it. Read the relevant press. Markets, products, technologies, processes are constantly morphing.

Longer range, where are the trends in general and specific to an industry? Industry research reports and seminars are good ways to predict future changes. Listen up.

So what?

Here are some real reasons to dig into significant shifts and communicate the details:

- A key customer is unhappy and talking to a competitor.
- The market for one of your high-profit products is about to start declining.
- One of your critical production processes is slowing down.
- A new competitor is entering the market with a stunning product at a lower price.
- A top executive is dissatisfied and beginning to look outside.
- Your payroll is starting to balloon for unknown reasons.
- One of your best-selling products is experiencing failures at customer sites.
- A forthcoming federal work law will add significantly to your taxes.
- You are getting an untrue rap for being a bad company to work for.

- Some of your new marketing messages are not well received.
- A key vendor is experiencing large financial failures.

Find the truth, determine the importance, and start communicating. Fast.

Who you gonna tell?

Start with your immediate staff. Rally them into helping to determine what actions to take, how and when. Some or all employees need to know. Be wary of hiding problems – your people will figure it out soon enough. "Don't tell" is often a bad path.

Who outside the company needs to know? Your board, vendors, and the community are good candidates. Sometimes the press should be told, particularly if remedial actions and apologies are a good thing to describe. Manage bad news before it manages you.

Others can include your advisors, bankers, shareholders, and government regulators.

What about upsides?

Not all change is negative. Some is very positive, including: higher than expected sales, hiring a well-known executive, a patent for brilliant new technology, obtaining a new major customer, a valuable acquisition. Communicate these events to the world!

What are you pretending not to know?

Hiding your head in the sands of change can suffocate your company. Kodak ignored the digital photography moment. The original American Airlines ignored the takeoff of Southwest. And Borders did not read the flow of Amazon into online book sales. RIP.

The bottom lines

Like radar. Scan for change, constantly. See shifts that have occurred, are occurring, and are likely to occur. Understand the impacts, and communicate to your team and others. Act accordingly. Hire a CCDO – Chief Change Detection Officer. Stay alive.

Leadership Lesson 36

Feeling scrambled? The one thing every great leader must do

Oppressive. The juggler with too many objects; an endless list of "to-do's;" a calendar packed with no sleep. Feelings of futility, an urge to keep working even harder, and little sense of real accomplishment. Oh, and killer stress. Now what?

The core issue is that we tend to view everything as of equal importance. High. Author Stephen Covey and WWII General (later U.S. President) Dwight Eisenhower taught us how to focus on the "important" vs. the "urgent." Today, that is not enough. Read on.

Your actions define your priorities. – Gandhi, India activist and leader

Driving forces

Why is it increasingly difficult to prioritize our own actions – and the activities of our organizations? Acceleration. The screaming velocity of business (and life) today. The volume and speed of transactions, interactions, and intersections. Add more competition, a worldwide market, and the Internet of Everything. A speed that is warping us.

Fear. Fear of failure, fear for our careers, fear of business (and personal) economic pressures. We try to outrun fear with frenzied action. Everything becomes important, everything becomes urgent, and all the overfilled spinning plates crash.

Time to learn a new path to effective prioritization. Now.

Must. Important. Urgent. Never.

Must? You mean that the important and the urgent might not include the must do's? True. Further, what is important to one of us might not be to another. And that which is urgent to one person, might not be to someone else. Even important and urgent things get mixed up and comingled.

Pareto knows. 20% of our actions create 80% of our results. So what is the 20% that really matters?

And, who is determining what the musts are? Unscramble the mass and mess of priorities with a few, simple rules.

Reality rankings

Here is an effective means to manage your tangled web of too many to-do's:

- First, delete everything that is not a must, important, or urgent. This alone, should leave the 20% that is worth any action.
- If something must be done no matter what, then add it to your list of priorities. Note the date by which the item has to be accomplished.
- Label the important items as such. Rate each item on a 1 to 3 scale as to its level of importance. Keep all the 1's and hide the remainder for another day.
- Get rid of all the urgent items unless they have a due date. Relabel those as important and assign a rating of 1 to 3. Keep only the 1's and hide the others for now.
- Put all the musts at the top of your list and order them by their due dates.
- Arrange the remaining important items by their due dates.
- At your weekly staff meeting, review the remainder of the list and ask them to help you rank, assign, and delegate the remaining items. Re-rank and review progress every week.
- When an item is completed, add a new one per the above method.

Isolate those items that you intend to do yourself. Review them every morning.

The bottom lines

Get unscrambled. Get prioritized. Learn how to deal with the must do's, the important actions, and the urgent items. Follow the rules for ranking, above. You will be taking care of only those things that really matter. Less stress, more success.

Leadership Lesson 37

The missing link – what is your higher standard?

Plateaued? You know that you have more capabilities and capacities in you. And in your organization. But you feel frozen. You have been successful several times. And are now coasting, along with your organization. Time to move forward.

Toward what? Think about these questions: what is another stretch in your career; what else motivates you; what is your higher purpose? In other words, "What is your higher standard?" How many others can you serve with your leadership capabilities?

A good goal is like a strenuous exercise - it makes you stretch.
- Mary Kay Ash, American businesswoman

What's next?

Time to move upward. Again. You have done it before both individually and organizationally. And the result has been the growth of yourself, your company, your organization.

You could shoot for a promotion, an expanded career elsewhere, some valuable new learning via courses or business mentors and coaches.

Another path is to focus on strengthening your company with new markets and products. And improve your organization with enhanced training. Acquire another company for more revenues, products, and profits. Growth.

Do list

Seven steps into a higher standard of being and behavior.

1. Dream and document – spend time clarifying your next move, your higher standard. Describe it in detail, discuss with others for feedback and more ideas. Keep reworking your "Dream Journal" until it resonates with you.

2. Establish goals – including milestones by date. What will you accomplish and when? What outcomes will you achieve? Find someone, perhaps a mentor or coach, who will hold you accountable for meeting your objectives.

3. Overcome fears – each time we climb into a higher ground, there is anxiety, doubt, and resistance. Again, discuss this fully with your "accountability partner." Be your own cheerleader and talk yourself out of giving up.

4. Note progress – when you are implementing your actions always capture every bit of progress and note it in your Dream Journal. Any time you are feeling blocked, read your progress list. Give yourself credit for lifting off from your plateau.

5. Clean up messes – so you make mistakes along the way. Fix them, learn from them, and keep moving. Talk about them with your accountability partner or mentor. Ask others for help. Keep moving forward, never look back.

6. Celebrate successes – anytime you have reached a milestone, give yourself credit. Celebrate and thank those who are helping you – even if it is one person who is helping you find a new position or career.

7. Pivot the plan – sometimes there is an obstacle that cannot be overcome. Instead of stopping, think about how you can modify your dream to make it more achievable. Hold a brainstorming session to help.

Grow, succeed, plateau, and repeat. Always.

Electrifying example

Elon Musk got Tesla on the road, fixing and pivoting along the way. Next, with some failures, he launched SpaceX into success. Now he is developing high-speed intercity travel,

Hyperloop. No plateauing for Elon. He keeps pushing to his higher standard.

The bottom lines

Successful. But not moving ahead. Feeling that something is undone. Time to build your next success by setting new goals. In your current role, a new career or job, something great for your organization. And yourself. See the seven steps, above. Go!

Leadership Lesson 38

How many assets are you wasting? More than you think

Too little? Truth is that we often have too many unused assets in our corporations, organizations, and small businesses – and are unaware of it. There is a cost associated with excess: cash, investment, space, staffing, real estate, and more. Look around.

Our financial friends (CFO, controller, accountant) see underutilized assets. They have a built-in aversion to waste. Ask them to build a list of the most unused and underused assets. Convert them to a better use. Including cash.

My mother was my biggest role model. She taught me to hate waste. – W. Edwards Deming, American engineer of high-quality, lean production for Toyota and others

Shopping list

Here are some key areas to look at for signs of waste:

<u>Excess inventories</u> – parts and raw materials that are lounging. Money is tied up in them and occupying valuable space.

Reduce or eliminate the excess. Sell it off for cash. Barter it for something you really need.

Unused real estate – land not being used nor appreciating. Entire buildings empty or partially utilized. Sell or lease the land to someone who can use it. Ditto, the empty and dead space buildings.

Declining values – some assets decline in value across time. If the asset is not needed, don't let it fully decline on your books. E.g., a large batch of a production material that is losing value and you do not need as much of it.

Consolidate assets – if you have two partially used buildings, move everything into one of them, and sell or lease the other building. This can be anything from a production area to an office space.

Technology gluttony – expensive technology for everything. It is too easy to overstuff ourselves with it. Get the expertise to determine what is needed for what purposes, understand all costs now and later, and get the real return on investment (ROI).

Overstaffing – payroll can be the single largest expense item. Optimize the use of your employees. Not to overwork nor unnecessarily terminate them. Simply utilize them more efficiently. Cross-training, better management, improved culture.

<u>Prevention</u> – why overpay for assets? Make sure that you are paying fair prices with good terms and conditions. Don't budget for a multi-month marketing program that fails in the first month. Be wary of a large purchase asset that could decline in value.

Real savings

EMC is a major supplier of IT services. They recently undertook to reduce their real estate expenses associated with 12M square feet of space for 50,000 employees. In a two-year period they cut 20%, or $80M, from their real estate portfolio.

Harvard research notes that virtually any department can cut its expenses by 10%.

Waste not, want not. – Benjamin Franklin, a U.S. Founding Father

The bottom lines

Excess. Too much real estate, too much staffing, too much production capacity, too much technology, too much inventory. Too much, period. Reduce, eliminate, consolidate. Find the weight, lose the bloat, gain the cash.

Leadership Lesson 39

No secret – Amazon reveals their 14 principles of leadership

Disclosed. Many organizations, both for-profit and not-for-profit, promote their vision, mission, and values. But, without strong leadership, the vision is only a vision. Why not promote the leadership principles of successful organizations? E.g., Amazon.

Amazon.com is very public and proud of the leadership principles that have governed their nova burst into corporate stardom. Who would have bet their beer money on a startup that 23 years ago started selling books online – and is now the 12th largest company in the United States?

Rules are not necessarily sacred, principles are. – Franklin D. Roosevelt, 32nd president of the United States

Amazon flows

Started in 1993, Amazon surpassed Walmart with the highest market value of any retailer in the U.S. Walmart took 53 years to reach that point – Amazon 23 years. Leadership.

Amazon is the third most valuable company in the world. And, after Walmart, the second largest employer in the U.S. Leadership.

As of 2017, per the Fortune 500 listings, Amazon is the 12th largest company in the U.S. based upon revenues. Leadership.

The secret is out

Go to **https://www.amazon.jobs/principles** and have a look at the 14 leadership principles that have guided this riches to more riches organization:

Customer obsession – Leaders start with the customer and work backwards. They work vigorously to earn and keep customer trust. They obsess over customers.

Ownership – Leaders are owners. They think long term and act on behalf of the entire company. They never say, "That's not my job."

Invent and simplify – Leaders expect and require innovation and invention from their teams and always find ways to simplify. They are not limited by, "Not invented here."

Are right, a lot – Leaders have strong judgment and good instincts. They seek diverse perspectives and work to disconfirm their beliefs.

Learn and be curious – Leaders are never done learning and always seek to improve themselves. They are curious about new possibilities and act to explore them.

Hire and develop the best – Leaders raise the performance bar with every hire and promotion. They recognize exceptional talent, develop more leaders, and coach others.

Insist on the highest standards – Leaders have relentlessly high standards. They drive their teams to deliver high quality products, services and processes.

Think big – Leaders create and communicate a bold direction that inspires results. They think differently and look around corners for ways to serve customers.

Bias for action – Leaders know that speed matters. Many decisions and actions are reversible and do not need extensive study. They value calculated risks.

Frugality – Leaders accomplish more with less. Constraints breed resourcefulness. There are no extra points for growing headcount, budget size, or fixed expense.

Earn trust – Leaders listen attentively, speak candidly, and treat others respectfully. They are vocally self-critical, testing themselves and their teams against the best.

Dive deep – Leaders operate at all levels, stay connected to the details, audit frequently, and are skeptical when facts and here-say differ. No task is beneath them.

Have backbone – Leaders are obligated to respectfully challenge decisions when they disagree, even when doing so is uncomfortable. Once a decision is made, they commit.

Deliver results – Leaders focus on the key inputs for their business and deliver them with the right quality and in a timely fashion. They rise to the occasion and never settle.

The bottom lines

Leadership principles. What are yours? Why not review Amazon's 14 principles and adopt those that will help your organization. After all, Amazon's work well. Very well.

Leadership Lesson 40

It's messy doing the right thing

Implication. That doing the right thing is always easy. Not. Often, taking the higher road is under adverse conditions. Choosing a contrary action has a cost. It requires integrity. Real leadership.

Amid complaints about its water usage, Coca Cola invested $30 million to reduce its production consumption of water by 25% and is involved in over 400 global water conservation projects. Additionally, the company has invested $5 billion in India to help clean up their drinking water. They are doing the right thing, even though it is a "muddy" project. Integrity.

It is always the right time to do the right thing. – Martin Luther King, civil rights activist

Who does the right thing?

Leaders and others. It is part of a good company culture. Doing the right thing is fundamental to creating and sustaining an effective, organizational value system. And it begins at the top.

<u>Leaders must lead</u> – if the leader is not consistently taking right action, employees see it. So do outsiders, including customers, vendors, and community members. One CEO found out that one of his employees was struggling with a low income. The CEO increased all employees' salaries to $70,000 per year. Every employee saw it – and felt it. The right thing was done – and then some.

<u>Rewards matter</u> – when leaders support employees to do right things with rewards, the values of the organization are upheld, emphasized, and strengthened. A known reward system for special right actions in challenging situations boosts morale and a willingness to do it again. Merely saying, "Thank you" in a public way works wonders.

<u>Flexible rules</u> – good leaders make certain that operating processes and procedures are not so rigorous that employees will avoid reaching out in a sensible way to take the path of right action. This is especially true when a contrary action will save a situation from becoming worse. Some organizations give employees the latitude to bend the rules within reason, based upon their own common sense.

<u>Real measures</u> – when leaders establish "make the numbers" (e.g., profits) as the only definition of success, much is missed. Doing the right thing is more powerful than doing things right. Right action supports stronger leadership, better teams,

effective communications, good interpersonal connections, and happy employees that help each other and customers.

<u>Appropriate apologies</u> – any leader who can admit that they did not do the right thing deserves the admiration of employees and others. Any good human can error in judgment. But to admit it and repair it is doing the right thing! One value noted in the mission statement of a southwestern company is, "We clean up our messes and do better."

Good leaders give us the latitude to do the right things even when it is messy. It's right.

And it is profitable

JUST Capital tracks companies that have a high focus on justice, ethics, and fairness. Most of these organizations (per the Russell 2000 index):
- Are more profitable
- Pay 20% more workers a living wage
- Created 1.8x more jobs
- Recycle about 3 times more waste
- Donate about 2 times as much of their profits to charity

The bottom lines

Messy. Doing the right thing is often contrary to the rules of a business. But it can build better organizations and create happier customers. And, it is more profitable in the long term. Great leaders do the right thing. Consistently.

175

Leadership Lesson 41

Cracks in the dashboard – fix it with better business metrics

Metrics. Dashboards. Key Performance Indicators (KPI's). Most of them tell us where we have been. Some tell us where we are. And fewer tell us where we are going. When we read them, we often react with one foot on the accelerator and one foot on the brake – and our business bus spins around on the freeway to nowhere.

Case. For years we saw the Income Statement and the Balance Sheet as our critical metrics. Problem: they tell us more about where we have been and a little about where we might be going. But only a few whiffs about whether we have enough fuel (cash) to go forward. Or not.

Cash. It was only in 1992 that the Cash Flow Statement was mandated as a critical metric for business health. Past. Present. Future.

Bye-bye paper, hello pixels

Once we could stop looking at disparate pieces of paper, and start looking at an IT-provided screen with multiple readings about business health, we can see a NASA-like, successful launch screen full of KPI's.

Problem. Many of these readings are past performance indicators. In fact, some are irrelevant. What matters last month's sales if there are no prospects for this month's business?

Leadership means forming a team and working toward common objectives that are tied to time, metrics, and resources. – Lieutenant General Russel Honore, American soldier

The new metrics

Here are the primary engines of business growth and profitability:

- Cash
- Markets
- Products
- Sales
- Workforce

What are a few KPI's that should be some of the measurement dashboards for each of these areas?

Cash – how much was generated and utilized last month; daily cash balance and its trend; what is the monthly projection for the next year; and where we can get more internally and externally, monthly.

Markets – monthly; revenue from each market (past, present, future); what is being spent for marketing in each market by product line; the cost to get a new customer; the cost to keep an existing customer; projected sales for upcoming products.

Products – what new products will be launched, when, their percent state of readiness; monthly revenues by product, past, current, projected (current and future products); product profitability; revenues from intentionally phase-out products.

Sales – monthly "Pipeline" (leads, prospects, orders), actual and projected; actual and estimated sales by products and markets; existing customer activity; new customer activity; top-ten customer activity; dormant customer activity; website activity.

Workforce – monthly counts by department; productivity; turnover and reasons; employee satisfaction; measures of company culture done by outside resources; training effectiveness.

Other areas for dashboard viewing include production, productivity, space utilization, customer satisfaction levels (e.g., Net Promoter Scores); and many more.

A few more things …

Peter Drucker, management expert noted, "What's measured, improves." Astoundingly, just 22% of companies have metrics to measure their innovation effectiveness.

Be more concerned about the content of the dashboard than its appearance; draw visible trend lines through all data; use outside dashboard software; don't forget online, social media, and Google info.

Use Big Data and AI to feed your dashboards. Best dashboards equal best businesses.

The bottom lines

Driving blind? Fix your company dashboard. Determine, implement, and measure all the best data that tracks daily, monthly performance (or lack thereof). That tells you and your staff the health of your company. Past, present, and future.

Leadership Lesson 42

Toxic cultures and the chemistry of effective leadership

Odious. Remember the experiments with sulfur in our high school chemistry labs? We might not recall the experiment, but the odor is an indelible memory. And, when we created a pleasant-smelling chemical ester, we will remember that as well. E.g., pineapple.

You might have heard that employees do not leave bad companies – they leave bad managers. Here is a contemporary extension of that idea: "Employees do not leave bad organizations – they leave bad cultures."

Company cultures have a certain, memorable "odor" in the sense of whether we are repelled or attracted by it.

The leader is the culture

For many years we have believed that we can fashion a company culture. Establish and follow great visions, missions, values. And there is truth in this. But, HR cannot do this unaided.

If organizational and company leaders do not live the desired culture on a daily basis, then the shape of the culture becomes an amorphous mass that is the sum of undirected behaviors within and among the employees.

Strong leaders consciously shape a culture based upon established and updated values. And these leaders visibly behave accordingly and ask others to do the same.

Turnover the turnover

What percent of your workforce leave the company each year? Per *Compdata*, Voluntary turnover (employees who were not terminated, but left on their own) increased from 15% to 19% between 2013 and 2017. Bad trend.

And, Gallup surveys continue to note that over 50% of U.S. employees are disengaged, 17% are actively making trouble, and 34% are engaged. And in a study by the *iOpener Institute for People and Performance,* engaged and enthusiastic employees:

- Stay five times longer in their jobs
- Are twice as productive
- Take 10 times less sick leave

What's the difference? Engaged employees are working in an irresistibly attractive culture – created by effective leaders. Intentionally.

Leaders of the culture

What is the chemistry of those leaders who build toxic-free cultures that attract and retain engaged employees? Among other things, these leaders:

1. Mentor, coach, teach and promote their people.
2. Lift and excite their employees.
3. Celebrate wins by acknowledging individuals and teams, regularly.
4. Encourage their employees to identify problems and help solve them.
5. Accept accountability for their own failures and don't blame employees.
6. Describe clearly what they want their people to produce.
7. Negotiate milestone dates with what is to be delivered and when, fairly.
8. See vulnerability as a real strength for themselves and employees.
9. Manage stress well for themselves and their teams.
10. Delegate effectively with clarity and mutual commitment.
11. Provide regular performance reviews with their employees.
12. Review programs and projects for progress, helping the teams improve.
13. Are approachable by their people.
14. Do not play favorites.

15. Value employees for their creativity and problem-solving
    skills.

Example. Remember Blockbuster Video? They failed because
of boardroom infighting over how to do a strategic deal with
Netflix. This leadership poison spread into the organization's
culture. Blockbuster busted. Netflix booming.

The bottom lines

Into the lab. Time to remove a toxic organizational culture that
drives good employees away. The positive chemistry of a great
leader can create a culture that attracts and retains great
people. End of high turnover and start of high productivity.
Happy employees. Happy customers.

Leadership Lesson 43

The dark side of hypergrowth

Exciting. Marketing programs are working. Sales are accelerating. Profits are growing. Production is ramping up. Staffing is climbing. The vision is coming true. And the organization is abuzz. Our future seems assured. Not necessarily.

What are the downsides of hypergrowth? There are several and all of them can be difficult – even for good leaders. It requires a delicate balance of managing within a narrowband of "not enough resources vs. excess resources." Especially for an organization that has never experienced an unplanned rocket ride of accelerating sales.

The excessive increase of anything causes a reaction in the opposite direction. – Plato, Greek philosopher

Never enough vs. too much

What can go wrong when sales-driven growth happens? Plenty – and in all areas of the organization:

Cash – dizzying growth requires cash and lots of it. To fund organizational growth, purchase inventories for production, acquire office and production space, pay outside resources for their services, to expand marketing for further growth. Always be looking for cash before you need it. Fall behind on cash and growth slows. Too much cash? Invest it or use it for strategic acquisitions.

Culture – perhaps the organization had a work environment that was conducive to getting started and rolling into some growth. Hypergrowth changes things. The pace of work accelerates, processes can get cloudy nor stand up to rapid expansion. More mistakes are made and stress levels climb. It is important for leaders to recognize this and to maintain an environment that is buoyant, rewarding, and still fun to be part of.

Organization – hiring quality people into the right positions at the right time is cost-critical. Labor is most often the highest expense. Not enough people can mean less production and more stress. Too many people means more cost and lower profits. Maintaining a constant labor planning process and productivity levels is fundamental. Particularly in a tight labor market. Having great HR organization is priceless.

Inventories – in a production setting having the right amount of inventory at the right time is another balancing act. Too much inventory raises costs and lowers profits. Too few materials slows production and order fulfillment, irritates customers, and slows revenue flow. A strong production planning team will work wonders – particularly if they are using the best IT tools available.

Service – you are shipping products or providing services at a furious rate. Customer installations are ramping up as planned. But if there are issues with customer training, support, problem resolution, slow service response time, something else pops up. Revenue drag. Customers can delay payment until problems are solved. Trust diminishes. Have a stellar customer support team in place. And they can after-sell, too.

Marketing – your marketing machine lit a fuse that is causing the growth explosion. Do not let them rest. Keep marketing going with a planned flow of new products and services. Add new markets and niches. Keep asking what existing and future customers want. Watch competition and stay ahead of them. In other words, momentum matters. Momentum builds more momentum. Even faster growth.

The company becomes a highly-tuned master of growth. Nonstop hypergrowth. Witness Apple, Amazon, Google.

The bottom lines

Hypergrowth. Exciting and dangerous. Great leaders balance the resources needed for high-growth. Not too many resources too soon. And not too few resources too late. No guesswork. Lead a growth team. Consciously, intentionally, early. Maximize opportunity.

Leadership Lesson 44

We admit our mistakes and clean up our messes

Mistake? Caused a problem with a customer, prospect, an employee, a vendor, or one of our communities? It happens. Pseudo-leaders try to cover a mistake. Real leaders admit it and then take care of the mistake. Righting a wrong. Doing the right thing.

Here are a few examples of companies that tried to ignore mistakes in 2016 alone:

- Yahoo had one of the largest hacking breaches known – but took two years to disclose it. At least 500 million user accounts were affected. Really bad PR followed by an acquisition by Verizon – at a reduced price.
- Mylan suffered from unfair, radical price hikes for its pharmaceuticals. A 400% hike for its life-saving EpiPen, plus similar hikes on seven other drugs. Result? Public ire, anti-trust lawsuits, and a stock fall of over 70%.
- Wells Fargo created 2 million unauthorized bank and credit card accounts over five years. The Consumer Financial Protection Bureau fined the bank $185 million.

Had these mistakes been admitted and cleaned up quickly, the cost would have been far less. Short and long term.

Run, don't walk

As soon as a mistake is known, deal with it. A mess grows like a forest fire and can get out of control. If it is leaked by consumers, employers, vendors, or others – and the lightning online press hears picks it up – it can be bad. Or lethal.

Good leaders will reveal the error, tell the truth, explain what happened, and offer restitution. Products are recalled, reworks are offered, monetary compensation is provided, substitutes are available. Whatever it takes to rectify the situation.

Result? Buyers are more forgiving, the public views the company more favorably, employees are relieved. A sense of fairness and good leadership envelopes the organization. Win-win.

Classic corrections

When the solid leaders of these example companies took action to rectify a problem, here are some results:

1. Johnson & Johnson dumped tainted Tylenol packages at a cost of $250M. This move saved the brand, which provided 17% of J&J's revenues.

2. Samsung spent several billion dollars to cover the cost of overheating batteries in the Galaxy Note 7. Next year the Galaxy Note 8 sales took off with strong reviews.
3. Volkswagen could not hide defective diesel engine tests and repaired the problem for $18 billion. After their stock hit a subsequent bottom, it continues to recover.
4. Mattel eliminated some nine million toys produced in China due to excessive lead in the paint. Cost was $30 million. Brand protected.
5. Tyson recalled 2.5 million pounds of chicken products. A labeling mistake failed to note that there was milk in the products. The label was fixed quickly. Cost unknown.

The point is that these were massive messes – but the companies involved stepped up at all costs to clean up the situation. Customers saved, jobs saved, reputation saved. In some cases the company saved.

A fix it culture

An organizational culture is established upon the values of the leadership. Good managers might do things right – but great leaders to the right thing. Always.

The bottom lines

Made a mess? Move swiftly to clean it up. Save customers, employees, time, and money. Don't hide a wrong for the wrong reasons. Do the right thing for the right reasons. Make this part of your organizational culture. Now and always.

Leadership Lesson 45

The cage of comfort and how to unlock it

Smooth. Business is great and things are going well. Steady sailing ahead. In the often quoted key character in Mad Magazine, Alfred E. Neuman , "What me worry?" So, what can go wrong? Everything.

Any part (or all) of a successful business can cause significant problems. Massive product failures, expensive marketing programs that didn't work, a competitor gets ugly. Often ignored until it is too late.

Nature doesn't care that you are comfortable, only that you evolve. – Dr. Harville Hendrix, Ph.D., American author

It can't happen to me

Lest you forget, here are some disasters that blew up comfortable companies:

Remember when major banks were "too big to fail"? In the 2008 Great Recession many came close to closing. Federal government action saved most of them, but some crashed – e.g., bye, bye Lehman Brothers. Scars remain on others.

Japanese automobile air bag producer, Takata, suffered the mother of all product failures in 2013 with 42 million cars recalled. Takata went bankrupt. Interestingly, in 1995, eight million cars were recalled due to faulty Takata seat belts. Encore?

General Electric was one of the Dow Jones stock market index of 30 stocks since 1907. G.E. did not mind its business. A pyramid of debt is forcing them to sell off major businesses. G.E. light bulbs are dimming. So is G.E.

American Airlines ignored Southwest Airlines move into low-cost, easy-access flights. Later, American headed into bankruptcy, was acquired by competitor USAir (who kept the name "American"), and now ignores nothing. Rough flight.

Kodak owned the photography industry's film and processing segment for decades. Ironically, Kodak invented the world's first digital camera – and then put it aside. They later brushed off the onslaught of digital photography. The Kodak moment is over.

The CEO of LifeLock, an identity theft prevention company, advertised his social security number to prove that LifeLock would prevent theft of his identity. It has now been stolen 13 times. And the FTC sued $12M for false advertising. Marketing bummer.

Tesla's reputation and financial condition has been negatively impacted by serious, unforeseen delays in the production of its new Model 3 automobiles. Further, the price of some 500,000 units on order has risen. Shocking.

Big successes turned into huge failures. While leaders were quietly caged by the comfort of those earlier successes. How do we unlock those cages? And, how do we prevent slipping into the comfort of success?

Swarming and shunning

If we are not too late, then unlock the cage of comfort and attack the core issues that we face. Build an attack team, dissect the problems, and form expert teams to swam the concerns with solutions.

Better yet, be aware of everything that is going on in the company (and outside it), anticipate problems before they happen, form barriers to failure, and shun anything that could go wrong.

The point is to never feel comfortable with success. Failure is lurking somewhere in the organization. Find it before it finds you. Vigilance.

The bottom lines

Comfortable with success? It's a warning for good leaders. The potential for big trouble is just around the corner. Always be looking for problems. Then solve them. Better yet, anticipate failures before they happen. Too successful to fail? A deadly belief.

Leadership Lesson 46

Are you hiring Work Ready employees? Really?

Available. Plenty of people ready to work, yet too few are "Work-Ready." Having only the job content skills, "Hard Skills," is not enough. There are four more capabilities of significance. Four more? Keep reading.

The four added capabilities are: effective communications abilities; cultural fit; supportive behaviors; leadership mindset (even if they have no high-level job title nor any people reporting to them). These are the "Soft Skills." So what?

Businesses understand increasingly that just knowing how to do a given job does not necessarily create an excellent employee – from CEO through every role in the organization. The four "Soft Skills" can make or break top performance. How?

E.g.

Here are some examples what happens due to inadequate skill sets:

When a given set of content skills are applied to the wrong job, then this mismatch likely will not produce the desired outcome – true of executive positions, too.

If an employee has the skill to delegate work, but cannot communicate well, then there is no effective delegation.

Expecting new hires to automatically fit into the existing culture of the company is a mistake. If they do not happen to match, then they can be a problem employee.

Given that a prospective hire does not have the behaviors to support strongly their job content skills, there is an increased chance they will fail the job.

If candidates don't have a bias to action, or an attitude of problem solving, or are unable to help motivate others, they lack a leadership mindset and are dependent.

And, if an existing employee is a candidate for a promotion or internal job change, will they still match the five areas of employee suitability: content skills, effective communications, cultural fit, supportive behaviors, and a leadership mindset?

Simple score

Here is an easy way to evaluate each of the five areas of capacities:

1. Job Content Skills: score their demonstrable job skills from 0 to 5 and have a threshold of at least 4 to further consider the candidate.

2. Effective communications: give them 0 to 5 points for their obvious abilities to speak, write, read, and (especially) to listen well – with a minimum acceptable score of 3.

3. Cultural Fit: before describing the company culture, ask candidates about their culture, values, beliefs. Then score them 0-5 re how well they can fit in. Minimum score of 3.

4. Supportive Behaviors: do they exhibit behaviors that will make them good members of teams – such as empathy for others? Score them from 0 to 5, with a minimum score of 3.

5. Leadership Mindset: even if the candidate will not have a manager or executive title, or a staff, do they have the mental characteristics of leaders? Score 0-5, minimum score of 3. However, if they will be a manager or executive, minimum score of 4 is essential.

Total score? Candidates must have a minimum score in each of five categories. Then, take a look at the sum of those scores to help make your choice. Get input from other interviewers. And trust your intuition.

Our work is the presentation of our capabilities. – Edward Gibbon, English author

The bottom lines

"Hard Skills" – knowing how to do a job is critical. So are "Soft Skills" – effective communications; cultural fit; supportive behaviors; leadership mindset. Find, evaluate, and hire real "Work-Ready" people who have both skill sets. Really.

Leadership Lesson 47

See 16 signs of Good Leader mutating into Bad Leader

Constantly. We read about good leaders who become great leaders. How often, though, do we hear about good leaders gone bad? Great leaders conquer stress. But bad leaders cave to stress. Why?

Having ridden through good times, they are unable to handle the strain of major challenges. It is easier to be a good leader in good times – but stress can force a fall from grace.

"In times of great stress or adversity, it's always best to keep busy, to plow your anger and your energy into something positive." – Lee Iacocca, former Chair and CEO of Chrysler Corporation

Meet "Bad Leader"

Here are 16 signals that Bad Leader is emerging from Good Leader. Bad Leaders:

1. Must know where employees are and what they are doing, always.

2.   Believe that they can do every job better than their employees.

3.   Push all blame for everything to the employees.

4.   Are feared by their employees.

5.   Cause their employees to feel depressed.

6.   Over-assert their authority.

7.   Are controlled by their stress.

8.   Do not know their numbers or value what their employees are creating.

9.   Avoid regular performance reviews with their employees.

10. Impose very task-oriented roles for employees.

11. Provide training that is rigid about how things must be done.

12. Are reluctant about delegating tasks to employees.

13. See vulnerability as a weakness.

14. When delegating, dictate how a task is to be done.

15. View their employees as robots to make money.

16. Are not leaders – they are poor managers at best.

Example: Al "Chainsaw Dunlap is a West Point graduate, but now a disbarred corporate executive. He is banned from serving as an officer of a publicly traded corporation in the United States. His widespread layoffs and accounting frauds have put him on several lists of the worst CEOs.

Meet "Good Leader"

Good Leaders build great teams that enjoy their careers, the work environment, and being part of something good.

1. Lift and excite their employees.
2. Celebrate wins by acknowledging individuals and teams, regularly.
3. Encourage their employees to identify problems and help solve them.
4. Accept accountability for their own failures and don't blame employees.
5. Describe clearly what they want their people to produce.
6. Will negotiate milestone dates with what is to be delivered and when.
7. Can see vulnerability as a real strength for themselves and employees.
8. Manage stress well for themselves and their teams.
9. Delegate effectively with clarity and mutual commitment.
10. Provide regular performance reviews with their employees.
11. Review programs and projects for progress, helping the teams improve.
12. Are approachable by their people.
13. Do not play favorites.
14. Mentor, coach, teach and promote their people.
15. Value employees for their creativity and problem-solving skills.
16. Are true leaders and highly respected.

Good Leaders have proven to be the standard for sustainable success.

Meet "Great Benefits"

1.4 million employees in 50,000 locations were surveyed by Gallup in 2013. Good Leaders enjoy:

- 22% better profitability.
- 21% more productivity.
- 37% less absenteeism.

The bottom lines

Understand. Good Leaders can become Bad Leaders – quickly. Stress is the typical turning point. The signals before the storm are visible. Learn them and pivot back to the many benefits of Good Leader. Quickly.

Leadership Lesson 48

One touch marketing is dead - long live multitouch

Silver bullet solution? Not in marketing today. The psychology of prospect attention suggests that most buyers need to be poked between six and eight times to get their attention. Call these "Touch Points." And touched in different ways. Why?

All of us are drowning in the influx of marketing messages. Who do you notice most? The ones that keep appearing in different kinds of media. From different angles. It is like fishing with different lures until you catch one. No one lure catches all.

"Marketing is a contest for people's attention." – Seth Godin, American entrepreneur and author

Seven X Seven

Theory – potential buyers need to be touched by our marketing message seven different times, each in a different way. This is when buyers typically will notice us.

Applied – here are some different ways that our seven messages can be transmitted:

<u>Word of mouth</u> – 64% of marketing executives believe word of mouth is the most effective form of marketing. Southwest Airlines focuses on developing happy customers so that they will "tell a friend" about Southwest.

<u>Social media</u> – clearly, using LinkedIn and other online media to post marketing messages in the form of ads, blogs, case studies, offers, etc. 75% of Coca-Cola's business is outside the U.S. They use LinkedIn to keep their world informed.

<u>Advertising</u> – in all of its many forms of newspapers, online, billboards, TV, radio, business cards on your auto windshield are still alive. Ford published three print ads with QR codes so that readers' phones could scan them to see a car in video action.

<u>Phone calls</u> – rather than pure cold calls, contacting a valid lead who wants more information via a scheduled phone call can succeed. Siemens uses pre-established leads to set appointments for phone calls that work.

<u>Face-to-face</u> – this timeless touch point builds markets and trust. College campuses are famous for it. Microsoft, Red Bull, and others hold campus marketing campaigns. Microsoft student-reps give product demos to fellow students on over 300 campuses.

<u>Email</u> – well-constructed email campaigns provide informative, educational material to target audiences can be a strong touch point. PayPal demonstrated this with a message to teach customers how to quickly split restaurant bills (and pay them) among friends.

<u>Direct mail</u> – yes, it is still here and working. Just check your mail box. Existing and former customers, and prospects are good targets. Honda successfully uses direct mail to market new cars, service appointment reminders, trade-in offers, and more.

There are more opportunities for multi-touch marketing: having a website, sponsoring events, press releases, publicity stories, success stories, educational events – to name some. The point is, we can be very creative about the form of our seven touch points. With prospects. And with existing customers – to help keep them as customers.

To whom …

Our intended touch point recipients can be (and should be) at different levels of their organization. Depending upon the situation, the CEO or COO, VP finance, leaders of purchasing, production, marketing, sales, facilities, engineering, and others. Whomever is a buyer or a buying influencer. At different times – or sometimes at the same time.

The bottom lines

Touch-points. A marketing must. Send your marketing message to your prospects at least seven times. Each in a different way. And to different people. Marketing is fishing for buyers. Use different lures and in different parts of the water. Land more business.

Leadership Lesson 49

Still struggling with "The Vision"? Take these steps to clarify it

Confusion. This is a major cause of an unclear company vision. What are some reasons for a muddy vision? Mixed messages within the vision, poorly stated, disconnected from the actual business, not well communicated. And frequently changed. Read more.

Clarity. A vision is an inspiring dream of where the organization is headed and what it is becoming. A mission states what the company does as a business, and for whom. A purpose explains what good the company is doing for the world around it.

Myth: any vision statement is a guarantee for automatic business success in large corporations and small businesses.

Truth: a vision must be clear, creative, compelling, concise, communicated. Unique and futuristic as well. And doable. Or nobody will buy into it – employees nor customers. No sale.

Vision vs. mission and purpose

To help understand the similarities and differences about a business vision, mission, and purpose, here are some examples:

> *Mattel's <u>vision</u>: "To be the premier toy brand, today and tomorrow."*

> *Apple's <u>mission</u>: "Apple is committed to bringing the best personal computing experience to students, educators, creative professionals and consumers around the world through our innovative hardware, software and Internet offerings."*

> *Johnson & Johnson's <u>purpose</u>: "Caring for the world, one person at a time."*

Eliminating the confusion about a vision alone will help strengthen it. But there is more.

Increasing clarity

The steps to further crystalizing your vision statement until is sharply in focus are straightforward – no magic needed. Here are some simple steps to strengthen your vision.

Once you have a clear vision, stop changing it. Vision is the foundation of the business and should be the least changing element. Purpose, mission, and values can change a bit more often.

Communicate your vision clearly and concisely in different ways, internally and externally – spoken and written. Don't hide or bury it. Be proud of it.

Make certain that your mission, purpose, values (and culture), goals, and strategy support your vision. Else the vision will not transition into reality.

Smudgy visions: lack a winning idea that differentiates the company from its competitors; tend to be mushy, trite, complex; difficult to communicate; are not forward looking; so improbable that people will not enroll in them.

Clarity affords focus. – Thomas Leonard, American businessman

Winning visions

Look how inspiring visions move big dreams into reality:

Amazon – "Our vision is to be earth's most customer-centric company; to build a place where people can come to find and discover anything they might want to buy online." Now King-Konging the entire retail industry – including grocers.

<u>Facebook</u> - "People use Facebook to stay connected with friends and family, to discover what's going on in the world, and to share and express what matters to them." 25% of the world's population is on Facebook.

<u>Google</u> – "To organize the world's information and make it universally accessible and useful." Revenues $90 billion in less than 20 years; global penetration; Google it.

Remarkably, these three organizations were birthed only a few years ago. Great visions can reach great velocity. Fast.

The bottom lines

Vision. From cloudy to clarity is a focal point in morphing visions into reality. Learn to strengthen your vision. And your organization and business. Eliminate confusion and strive for a simple but powerful vision. Get help from your team. Start now.

Leadership Lesson 50

No problems? Create some in 7 easy steps

No problem. Everything in the business seems calm. No trouble in sight. Things seem to be running themselves. Sit back and relax. In the meantime, there is a fire in the foundation. And you do not know about it. Ignorance.

The velocity of business continues to accelerate. Things can go wrong at a much higher speed than before. Remaining oblivious to constant shifts in products, processes, and people is an opening to oblivion for your business. Wake up.

Kodak, American Airlines (the original company), and Blockbuster. What do they have in common? Read on.

No problem in sight

All three companies played "business as usual" and failed:

- Kodak ignored digital photography, even though they had invented the first digital camera. They refused to let go of their brick and mortar film processing business.

- American Airlines ignored competition, including better managed USAir, who acquired bankrupt American and kept the name "American Airlines").

- Blockbuster ignored the possibility of distributing movies via the Internet. Netflix grabbed the opportunity and showed how to do it.

Many other businesses, large and small, have coasted out of existence in a fog of "not knowing."

7 ways to create problems (if you do not have any)

Ignoring any and all aspects of a business is ignorance in action:

1. Ignore innovation – do not foster creativity, reward it, spend on it, hire people who are good at it, or make it a high priority. Exclude it from your culture. Some competitor will take care of it for you.

2. Ignore employees – meet with them only when you must, never ask for their opinions, pay them at substandard rates, show no interest in their personal lives, and do not let them know what is happening in the business.

3. Ignore cash – fly financially by the seat of your pants, do not read cash flow statements, just believe that sales

equals cash, don't worry about excess resources, above all never ask for a cash flow projection.

4. Ignore marketing – fixate on sales and hope that they continue, kid yourself and think that marketing and sales are the same, assume that your products are so good that they will sell themselves.

5. Ignore organization – stop hiring good people and go for mediocrity, put a hold on all training, do not offer performance incentives, allow your facilities to deteriorate, and micromanage everyone.

6. Ignore strategy – forget planning or only do it annually instead of continuously, act as though you have unlimited resources, unlink your actions from your goals, assume that there is no competition.

7. Ignore fundamentals – just let your vision, purpose, mission, and culture drift. Then you won't have any, or you will have too many – which is just as bad. And, do not bother to set goals. It is too much work.

If you have ignored everything successfully, you will not need to worry about the business – because you will not have a business. Retired.

The bottom lines

No problems? You can create some by simply ignoring the business – until you no longer have a business. Better yet, always be looking for challenges and you will find some. Then solve them to build a better business. Do it quickly – the market is moving.

Leadership Lesson 51

Bumpy or smooth? The road from "Dream" to Done".

Brainstorm. You have an idea for a new product or service. You might be an entrepreneur with a startup business. Or, more likely, an "intrapreneur" – an entrepreneur inside a larger organization. In either case, don't build the idea. Yet.

Before rushing to implement the idea, avoid a bad ride to the marketplace. Instead, take a little time to create a smoother path to success. Answer a few questions to clarify the idea and its implementation.

From *Inc. Magazine,* here are some of the worst product ideas of all time: New Coke, Ford's Edsel, Apple Newton, Heinz Purple Ketchup, Cheetos Lip Balm, Google Glass. Lost cost? Too much.

The power is in the question

Answer these ten questions to confirm your idea. Or kill it before wasting resources. Senior executives will ask these same questions before making an investment in the dream:

<u>Background and Opportunity</u> – what gave rise to the idea in the first place? What opportunity does it create? Why hasn't it been done before? Why is this idea better?

<u>Problem</u> – what need does the idea address? Where is the need, how large is it, and how important is it? What are the negative impacts of this problem?

<u>Solution</u> – how is the problem solved in a general view? What is new about this solution vs. others that have been tried before? Is the solution documented in detail?

<u>Strategic Fit</u> – in what ways does the idea support the vision, mission, values, goals, and strategy of the existing or new business? How could it damage the business?

<u>Buyers</u> – who and where is the market? What are their needs? Proof? What about competition? How many products can be sold at what cost and price? When?

<u>Resources</u> – what will be needed to implement the idea, start to finish? Monetary investment, staffing, capital equipment, materials, facilities, IT?

<u>Organizational Impact</u> – if implemented, what parts of the organization will be effected? In what ways, positive or negative? Could this idea be done outside the organization?

<u>Milestones</u> – what are the key events that must take place, when, and where? What is the critical path to completion? When is financial breakeven? What can go wrong?

<u>Project Management</u> – who are the people, existing and new hires, that will be needed to implement the idea on time? Who is the leader? Are there alternatives?

<u>Benefits</u> – how does the company benefit? Customer experience, process streamlining, employee experience? Profitability? Are there any negative consequences?

And, these are the same questions that investors will ask a startup business. Deeply.

And a few more questions …

What will happen if we do not implement this idea? Can we sell or license the idea to someone else? Can it be patented? What is the biggest risk?

What would happen if we spend the same amount of money and other resources on a different idea? Or, the same amount of money to accelerate something that is already working? What else do we need to know?

And, one of the best questions ever in nearly every situation: "What are we pretending not to know?"

The bottom lines

Risk. It is pervasive in new ideas. Good questions minimize the risk of implementing bad ideas. Asking these ten fundamental questions can clear the road for a better ride to success. Take a little time to avoid a big failure. First.

Leadership Lesson 52

No doors in your organizational silo? How to get in (and out)

Silo. That part of an organization which is cut off, isolated, not a collaborator, and refrains from teamwork. More interested in self-preservation than the welfare of the company. Does not allow information to flow into nor out of the organization easily. Frozen.

It is a leadership issue – both the leader of the silo and the leader of the broader organization. Silos taint the remainder of the organization, slow down progress, play political games, and waste resources.

"At Cisco, we're training leaders to think across silos." – John T. Chambers, former Executive Chairman and CEO, Cisco Systems, Inc.

How damaging can a silo be?

In 2014, General Motors recalled some 20 million vehicles. Among other reasons, failed ignition switches were blamed for 51 deaths and many injuries.

An internal audit by a former federal prosecutor pinned the cause on "information silos" – the failure of employees to communicate across departments. Or among themselves.

The cost? $4.1 billion for over 4,000 death and injury claims – and repairs to the millions of cars. A brutal failure of organizations and individuals living in their silos. Oh, and leadership failure.

Knock, knock

What is going on inside a silo? Here is a look:

Group dogma – the group begins to think as one; leaders are not questioned; outside ideas are rejected; the group is always right; blind spots form; politics take over; creativity dies.

Blurry vision – the direction of the company is ignored; members of the silo know best; the overall organization's mission is subservient to the unstated mission of the silo; chaos reigns.

Duplicate actions – poor communications within a silo can result in a project being done twice by the same organization; wasted resources; other projects suffer; costs go up.

Scrambled priorities – the members of a silo lose sight of priorities; worse, there are no priorities; miscommunicated and misunderstood priorities; the overall priorities of the company are ignored; everything is late.

Online amplifier – the Internet can make it worse; online silos develop; an email clique forms; others are cut out; communications take place only with the silo; problems expand faster; silos build inside silos; productivity takes a hit.

Collaboration is essential in business, more than ever. Within a company and its organizations. And outside the company. Silos suffocate teamwork. Stop it.

Sweeping out the silo

Once a damaging silo has been uncovered, begin at the top of it – the leader(s). Educate them on the damage that siloed information can cause. Show them the advantages of appropriate, free-flowing information. And train employees how to rightly share information – and to accept input from others outside their organization.

Re-address the company's vision, mission, and values. Demonstrate how taking down the silos supports them. Build an organizational culture that fosters information sharing, teamwork, and collaboration.

Establish broad, common, shared goals for the organization. Align priorities accordingly. If necessary, remove silo-builders from the organization. Better to motivate, incent, and reward those who exemplify a healthy sharing of information, resources, and ideas.

The bottom lines

Stop silos. These self-contained, isolated, groups within a company or organization cause great damage. Their hallmark is to control information flow into and out of their own domain. Weak teamwork, no collaboration, and wasted resources. Take steps to break down silos with education and incentives. Revitalize your vision. And the business.

How to Order More Books

The author, Tom Zender, hopes that you enjoyed this book.

Additional copies of both books in this series by Tom Zender are available:

The Bottom Lines 2016: 52 Unforgettable Lessons in Leadership

The Bottom Lines 2017: 52 More Motivating Lessons in Leadership

The Bottom Lines 2018: 52 More Memorable Lessons in Leadership

The Bottom Lines 2019: 52 More Important Lessons in Leadership

They can be ordered at www.amazon.com in both the print and digital e-book versions.

Contact the Author:

Tom Zender

tomzender@me.com

www.tomzendermentor.com